Day Walks on the Isle of Skye

20 ROUTES ON THE WINGED ISLE

Vertebrate Publishing, Sheffield
www.v-publishing.co.uk

Day Walks on the Isle of Skye

20 ROUTES ON THE WINGED ISLE

Helen & Paul Webster

Day Walks on the Isle of Skye

20 ROUTES ON THE WINGED ISLE

 First published in 2022 by Vertebrate Publishing.

Vertebrate Publishing, Omega Court, 352 Cemetery Road,
Sheffield S11 8FT, United Kingdom.
www.**v-publishing**.co.uk

A CIP catalogue record for this book is available from the British Library.

ISBN 978-1-83981-151-7

Front cover: **Old Man of Storr** *(route 4).*
Back cover: **Quiraing** *(route 3).*
Photography by Paul and Helen Webster unless otherwise credited.

All maps reproduced by permission of Ordnance Survey on behalf of The Controller of Her Majesty's Stationery Office. © Crown Copyright. 100025218.

Design by Jane Beagley, production by Cameron Bonser.
www.v-publishing.co.uk

Printed and bound in Europe by Latitude Press.

Vertebrate Publishing is committed to printing on paper from sustainable sources.

Contents

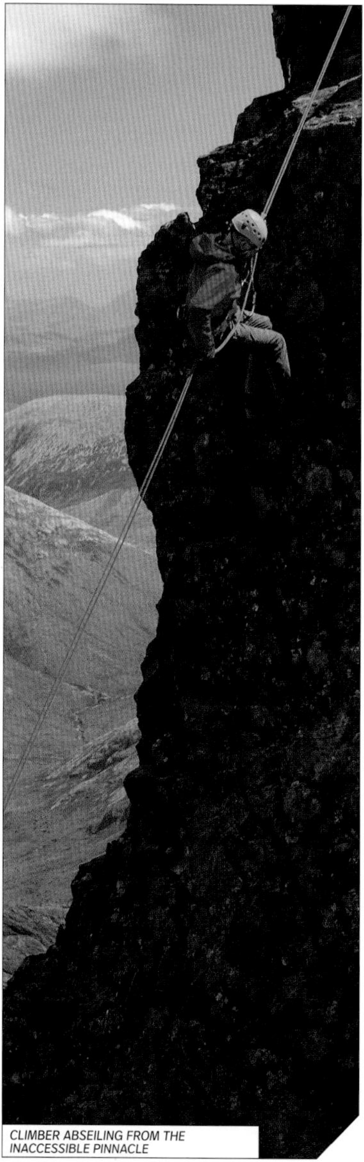

CLIMBER ABSEILING FROM THE INACCESSIBLE PINNACLE

Trotternish & the Braes

North-West Skye

Glen Brittle & Sligachan

South Skye & the Isle of Raasay

Day Walks on the Isle of Skye

AREA MAP & ROUTE FINDER

CLEAT AND BEINN EDRA FROM THE QUIRAING

Introduction

Crossing the sea to the Isle of Skye, whether by bridge or boat, is a moment of excitement and anticipation. The landscapes of the mainland Highlands may be superb, but the Isle of Skye has always had a special magic all its own.

For many, the remarkable Black Cuillin are the main draw on Skye. Formed by an ancient volcanic eruption, the dark gabbro and basalt rocks of this imposing mountain range have eroded and splintered to form Britain's ultimate playground for mountaineers. This book details the ascents of the easier of these peaks, but the rocky terrain, route finding and scrambling make them unique in Scotland and a satisfying challenge. Just reaching the foot of the Inaccessible Pinnacle and watching the climbers inching up this dramatic fin of rock and abseiling off it is an experience to treasure. There's so much more to Skye's landscapes than the Cuillin, however. In the north, the Trotternish peninsula is dominated by a remarkable landslipped ridge, presenting a sheer escarpment below, which are the iconic rock features of The Storr and the Quiraing. Hillwalkers can head to the summits above for views unseen by the mass of visitors below.

Away from the mountains, Skye's coastline is a revelation to many visitors. Towering cliffs, natural arches, sea caves and stacks are waiting to be discovered far from the island's roads, giving the chance to see white-tailed eagles, otters and even whales. Telltale signs of past cultivation provide a glimpse into the life of previous generations, while the ruins of cleared villages tell of the cruelties of the past. Following the walks in this guidebook will get you away from the beaten track, but taking a trip across to the neighbouring Isle of Raasay truly feels like a different world. Here you can climb to the flat top of the volcanic plug of Dùn Caan for a different kind of island adventure.

One of the Gaelic names for Skye is *Eilean a' Cheò* – the island of mist – and with its position off the west coast, Skye gets its share of dramatic weather. Combined with the rugged landscape, this can make walking here a serious proposition. Paths are often boggy or rocky – and on some routes, non-existent. The Cuillin, in particular, demands route-finding skills beyond those needed for hillwalking elsewhere. This is a landscape which needs to be treated with the utmost respect.

Helen & Paul Webster

About the walks

The walks in this book range between 3.5 and 14.5 miles (5.6 and 23.3 kilometres) and will take around three to ten hours at average walking speed without allowing for stops. The walks are arranged by area, and roughly in order of increasing difficulty within each area.

Don't be fooled into thinking some of the short distances on the mountain routes mean they will be easier or quicker walks. The terrain in the Cuillin is the toughest and rockiest in the UK which means slow going and difficult route finding in places.

None of the walks are signed or waymarked throughout, so the ability to read a map is essential. Be prepared for some pathless terrain requiring good navigation skills, particularly in poor weather. For the mountain walks, previous hillwalking experience is assumed.

Navigation

The islands of Skye and Raasay are covered in full by a number of Ordnance Survey (OS) Explorer 1:25,000 or OS Landranger 1:50,000 maps, while Harvey produce two maps covering the Cuillin and Trotternish in their 1:25,000 Superwalker range.

This book includes OS mapping as well as the route descriptions; however, it is always recommended to carry the relevant map so that you can navigate to safety if you need to leave the intended route. You should also carry a compass and be able to navigate using it on those routes. On the Cuillin the magnetising, high iron content of the rock makes compass readings very unreliable, particularly near the ridge itself; consider taking a GPS device and take great care with map reading and route finding on the ground.

The routes in this book are covered by the following maps in the OS 1:25,000 Explorer series:

407 Skye: Dunvegan
408 Skye: Trotternish & The Storr
409 Raasay, Rona & Scalpay
410 Skye: Portree & Bracadale
411 Skye: Cuillin Hills
412 Skye: Sleat

GPS & mobile phones

A GPS and/or mobile phone with OS-quality mapping installed on the device can be very useful, particularly in the Cuillin where navigation is notoriously difficult. Use a GPS to pinpoint your exact position on the map, or for checking against a downloaded route.

Many parts of Skye have little or no mobile phone signal, and be aware that batteries can fail on long or cold days; carry back up batteries, leave phones in airplane mode to prolong battery life, and tell someone where you are going and when you plan to get back.

Safety

Well-fitting walking boots will provide the protection and grip your feet need on the rougher routes. Trail shoes may be adequate in dry conditions on some routes but in general this area is notoriously boggy, and you should always expect some areas of wet ground. Similarly, always carry waterproofs, spare clothing including a hat and gloves on mountain walks (even in the summer), food and drink, and consider taking a torch and first aid kit.

Sunscreen and a sun hat should be taken in the summer. Midges can be an annoyance during the high summer months, repellent and/or a midge-net are useful. The tiny insects prefer damp, still weather and can often be avoided on hills or cliffs which are high enough to catch a strong breeze, and by steering clear of areas near placid water, particularly in the evening. Ticks, which can spread Lyme disease, are found in this area; carry a tick remover and check yourself at the end of the day. Long trousers and sleeves, light coloured clothing and avoiding walking through bracken are all good strategies. If you are bitten and then develop a 'bullseye' reaction at the bite spot, experience cold-like symptoms or feel unwell, seek medical advice.

Skye's weather can be remarkably fickle – locals know they may encounter four seasons in one day. Always check the weather forecast (including the mountain forecast for the higher routes) and be prepared for cold, windy and wet weather. Know how to navigate in low cloud and fog but in summer also plan for heat and strong sun. Sometimes the best decision can be to turn back – keep an eye on the weather and change plans if need be.

WINTER CONDITIONS

The walks are described for summer conditions only. Winter walking comes with its own challenges and dangers. The days are short; a head torch and spare batteries should be part of your kit. For the mountain walks when snow and icy conditions are forecast you must carry, and be adept in the use of, crampons and an ice axe. Check the Scottish Avalanche Information Service for current avalanche risks, plan your route accordingly and be prepared to change it. Navigation can be much harder when there are no paths visible on the ground. Attending a winter skills course is highly recommended, or at least go with more experienced people until you have the skills. Ensure that you have enough warm clothes and tell someone where you plan to go.

RESCUE

In case of an emergency dial **999** and ask for **Police** and then **Mountain Rescue**. Where possible give a six-figure grid reference of your location or that of your casualty. If you don't have mobile reception try to attract the attention of others nearby. The standard distress signal is six short blasts on a whistle every minute.

EMERGENCY RESCUE BY SMS TEXT

In the UK you can also contact the emergency services by SMS text – useful if you have low battery or intermittent signal. You need to register your phone first by texting '**register**' to **999** and then following the instructions in the reply. **Do it now** – it could save yours or someone else's life. **www.emergencysms.net**

Bothies

Bothies are unlocked shelters in remote locations throughout Scotland where hillwalkers, climbers and mountain bikers are able to spend the night. There are three on Skye (Camasunary, Ollisdal and The Lookout at Rubha Hunish) and Taigh Thormoid Dhuibh at the north end of Raasay. They range from rough stone shelters, an old coastguard watch room, to a purpose-built new property with several rooms. The Mountain Bothies Association is a registered charity taking care of around 100 bothies across the UK. Visit **www.mountainbothies.org.uk** for more information.

Roads & parking

Many of the roads on Skye are single track with regular, usually signed, passing paces. Pull over into passing places on your side of the road to allow oncoming vehicles to pass, and also to allow traffic behind you to pass – regularly check mirrors as well. Most roadside land is unfenced and livestock, in particular lambs in spring and summer, are an added hazard.

Never park in passing places or block access gates or tracks. Always ensure there is sufficient road space to allow wide emergency vehicles to pass and respect spaces reserved for mountain rescue vehicles. In recent years visitor numbers to Skye have increased and, while infrastructure catches up, parking can be difficult in some locations. Consider public transport options or arrive early (or late) and be prepared with a back-up plan for a different location if you cannot safely park.

THE CUILLIN FROM ACROSS GLEN BRITTLE

Scottish Outdoor Access Code

See **www.outdooraccess-scotland.scot** for more details.

TAKE RESPONSIBILITY FOR YOUR OWN ACTIONS

» Care for your own safety

» Keep alert for hazards

» Take special care with children

RESPECT PEOPLE'S PRIVACY AND PEACE OF MIND

» Do not act in ways that might annoy or alarm people, especially at night

HELP LAND MANAGERS AND OTHERS TO WORK SAFELY AND EFFECTIVELY

» Keep clear of land management operations like harvesting or tree-felling

» Avoid damaging crops

» Leave gates as you find them

CARE FOR YOUR ENVIRONMENT

» Don't disturb wildlife

» Take your litter away with you

KEEP YOUR DOG UNDER PROPER CONTROL

» Take special care if near livestock or during the bird breeding season

» Always pick up after your dog

How to use this book

This book should provide you with all of the information that you need for an enjoyable, trouble-free and successful walk. The following tips should also be of help:

- We strongly recommend that you invest in the relevant OS map for the walk. These are essential even if you are familiar with the area – you may need to cut short the walk or take an alternative route.
- Choose your route. Consider the time you have available and the abilities and level of experience of all members of your party – then read the Safety section of this guidebook.
- We recommend that you study the route description carefully before setting off. Cross-reference this with your map so that you've got a good sense of general orientation in case you need an escape route. Make sure that you are familiar with the symbols used on the maps.
- Get out there and get walking!

CAMAS DARAICH

Maps, descriptions, distances

While every effort has been made to maintain accuracy within the maps and descriptions in this guidebook, we have had to process a vast amount of information and we are unable to guarantee that every single detail is correct. Please exercise caution if a direction appears at odds with the route on the map. If in doubt, a comparison between the route, the description and a quick cross-reference with your map (along with a bit of common sense) should help ensure that you're on the right track.

Note that distances have been measured off the map, and map distances rarely coincide 100 per cent with distances on the ground. Please treat stated distances as a guideline only. Ordnance Survey maps are the most commonly used, are easy to read and many people are happy using them. If you're not familiar with OS maps and are unsure of what the symbols mean, you can download a free OS 1:25,000 map legend from **www.ordnancesurvey.co.uk**

Here are a few of the symbols and abbreviations we use on the maps and in our directions:

ROUTE STARTING POINT

SHORTCUT

ROUTE MARKER

OPTIONAL ROUTE

ADDITIONAL GRID LINE NUMBERS TO AID NAVIGATION

KM/MILE CONVERSION CHART

Metric to Imperial

1 kilometre [km]	1,000 m	0.6214 mile
1 metre [m]	100 cm	1.0936 yd
1 centimetre [cm]	10 mm	0.3937 in
1 millimetre [mm]		0.03937 in

Imperial to Metric

1 mile	1,760 yd	1.6093 km
1 yard [yd]	3 ft	0.9144 m
1 foot [ft]	12 in	0.3048 m
1 inch [in]		2.54 cm

Scottish place names

Many of the place names on Skye and the words used to describe the landscape derive from the Gaelic language with a good smattering of Norse reflecting the past settlers of the island. Here is a short glossary of some of the words you may encounter.

àirigh .... shieling or summer shelter
allt .... stream
baile .... town or settlement
bàn/bhàn .... white
beag .... small
bealach .. mountain pass, col or shoulder
bein/beinn ...... hill, mountain or peak
brae .... slope
burn .... stream
càrn/chàrn .... stony hill
clais .... gorge or ravine
cnoc .... small hill or knoll
coire .... corrie
creag .... crag, rock or cliff
dearg .... red
druim .... ridge
dubh .... black or dark
dun .... fort
eas .... waterfall
fada .... long
fasgadh .... shelter
fraoch .... heather
glas .... grey or green
làirig .... pass
loch .... lake
lochan .... small lake
meall .... rounded hill
meikle/mòr/mhòr .... big
mullach .... summit
ruadh .... red
sgurr/sgorr .... peak
srath/strath .... valley
stùc .... pinnacle, peak
tigh/taigh .... house

VIEW OVER TORRIDON FROM BLÀBHEINN

Section 1

Trotternish & the Braes

Trotternish is one of the most spectacular landscapes in Britain. The great ridge which forms its backbone is the longest on Skye, and its unique eastern escarpment has been broken by Europe's largest landslide into a remarkable landscape.

The coastline is equally spectacular. While the Kilt Rock and its waterfall are well known, much of the rest of the coastline is bristling with sea stacks and pinnacles, its hidden features revealed only by walking; Rubha Hunish, the northernmost peninsula, is regularly visited by minke whales in the summer.

The Braes region to the south has a similar feel to Trotternish, but on a smaller scale; it was here that crofters fought police during the Highland Clearances in the long struggle for security of tenure. Between Trotternish and the Braes is Portree, Skye's picturesque and bustling capital.

VIEW FROM THE STORR

ON BEN TIANAVAIG

APPROACHING THE SUMMIT

01 Ben Tianavaig 5.6km/3.5 miles

This diminutive coastal peak offers rewards far beyond the effort required to make the ascent.

Camustianavaig » Creagan na Sgalain » McQueen's Rock » Ben Tianavaig » McQueen's Rock » Camustianavaig

Start

Lay-by at Tianavaig Bay, Camustianavaig, south of Portree. GR: NG 508389.

The Walk

Well away from the usual tourist trail of Skye hotspots and overlooked by mountaineers, Ben Tianavaig deserves to be regarded as a classic shorter hill walk. It can be climbed in half a day and is a wonderful place to watch the sunset. Look out for white-tailed eagles which are plentiful here, or for dolphins passing through the Sound of Raasay far below.

The route starts from the beautiful, pebbly bay at Camustianavaig, a peaceful hamlet situated off the Braes road. The path climbs quickly and then hugs the coast, giving a fairly gentle ascent along a ridge that plunges steeply to the sea on your right; frequent stops are needed to appreciate the vista back over Tianavaig Bay to the distant Cuillin peaks. While the path is narrow and near the cliff edge at times, the going is on short-cropped turf and is unusually dry underfoot for Skye.

The escarpment leads up to a couple of rocky steps, but they are easily negotiated, or passed to the left. The summit trig point reveals views over Portree Bay and along the Trotternish peninsula beyond.

An alternative, more adventurous and partly pathless descent meanders steeply down the cliffs through an atmospheric forest of rock pinnacles, but returning the same way is no hardship with those wonderful views ahead. After the walk, leave time to explore the bay which is a haunt of herons and otters.

BEN TIANAVAIG

DISTANCE: 5.6KM/3.5 MILES » **TOTAL ASCENT**: 392M/1,286FT » **START GR**: NG 508389 » **TIME**: ALLOW 3 HOURS
MAP: OS EXPLORER 410, SKYE: PORTREE & BRACADALE, 1:25,000 » **REFRESHMENTS**: AROS CENTRE, NEAR PORTREE; CAFE ARRIBA, PORTREE » **NAVIGATION**: STRAIGHTFORWARD; CARE NEEDED NEAR CLIFFS. ALTERNATIVE RETURN ROUTE REQUIRES CAREFUL MAP READING AND IS ROUGH UNDERFOOT.

Directions - Ben Tianavaig

S From Portree, the sheltered settlement of Camustianavaig is reached by heading south along the A87, taking the first turn on the left signed *Braes*, then following signs for *Camustianavaig* to reach the lay-by at the back of the bay where there is a picnic table. Start by **heading left as you face the sea to walk along the road**. **Turn right** at a red post box and immediately **take the path** (signed *Hill Path*) that heads up to the left of the gate. Climb up between fences to soon leave the houses behind and pass through rowan trees. Beyond the fences **bear right** on a faint path to climb uphill diagonally. When the gradient eases, reach a fork in the path.

2 **Branch right** at the fork. Keep above the steep cliff of Creagan na Sgalain; there are great views down to the sea and Tianavaig Bay below. The path is narrow in places and care is needed near the cliff edge, especially in blustery weather.

3 Round the corner and **keep climbing** and **follow the edge of the escarpment** known as McQueen's Rock. (Staying by the cliff edge offers the best coastal views but there is also an alternative just to the left.) **Climb a couple of easy, rocky steps** as the route continues uphill; again these can be bypassed if required. Almost all of the Isle of Raasay is in view to the right. Keep an eye out for porpoises and dolphins, which can often be spotted moving through the narrows. **Keep to the cliff edge** and continue climbing; the trig point on the 413m summit of Ben Tianavaig eventually comes into view.

4 The views from the summit back to the Cuillin Hills and the Broadford Red Hills are spectacular on a clear day. Portree and its harbour and bay are suddenly revealed as are stunning views up the easterly coastline of the Trotternish peninsula to the north of Portree. The huge pinnacle of the Old Man of Storr stands out against the skyline and it's worth hanging around to see if you can spot the white-tailed eagles which nest nearby. From the summit*, the easiest way back is to initially **retrace the outward route** back down over McQueen's Rock.

* It is possible to make a **more difficult return route** (not included in the times or distance given). From the summit, **continue along the escarpment for 400m** until it is possible to **descend to the right**. From here, a rough descent can be made down the grassy valley of the An Ceam Dubh beneath Ben Tianavaig's cliffs. Once opposite a prominent, flat green pasture right down by the sea, you can work your way down the very steep, heathery slopes to

reach it. A narrow path then leads **south** along the coast; it soon **ascends** to keep above the shore. As the southern end of Ben Tianavaig is rounded, the slope becomes very steep, but the path cuts across it and gives a practical route. Beyond this airy section, the shore is reached at Camustianavaig.

5 **Bear right** on the more direct alternative path instead of following the cliffs around Creagan na Sgalain to soon regain the path down through the trees and between the houses to reach the road. There are great views towards the Cuillin all the way back down.

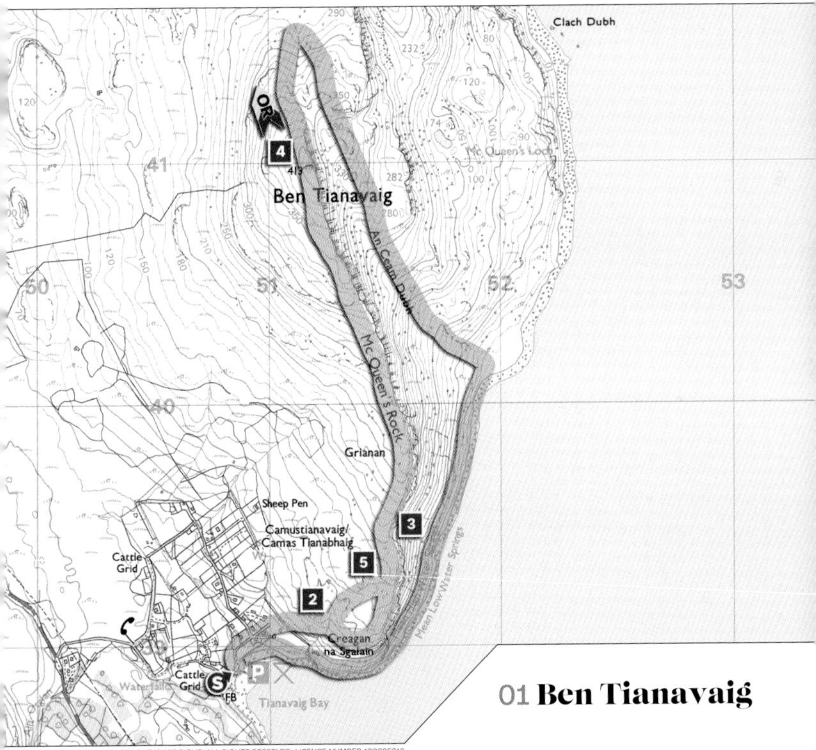

01 **Ben Tianavaig**

SEA STACK OFF RUBHA HUNISH

02 Rubha Hunish

8.4km/5.2 miles

Skye's northernmost headland is a real hidden gem, remarkable for both its landscape and wildlife.

Kilmaluag » The Lookout » Rubha Hunish » Meall Deas » Erisco coast » Loch Cleat » Kilmaluag

Start

Car park off the A855, west of Kilmaluag. GR: NG 423743.

The Walk

While the Trotternish peninsula is renowned for iconic landscapes like the Old Man of Storr and the Quiraing, this walk out to its northernmost point reveals a far less known but equally magical landscape. The walk begins on moorland before climbing to reach The Lookout, a bothy atop dramatic cliffs of fluted basalt columns. The bothy was once a coastguard lookout for watching ships passing through The Minch, but today it makes a great shelter for a break with amazing views of the sea and the Outer Hebrides beyond. Please help maintain it by carrying out any rubbish you find here.

Just below the bothy, a rocky path offers a descent to the hidden world below the cliffs. Reaching the headland on this path involves a scrambly descent of a rocky staircase, needing good footwear and a bit of a head for heights, but once down on the Hunish there are sea stacks, arches and *geos* (deep inlets) to explore. Formed when sea levels decreased at the end of the last ice age, this raised beach was once farmed by residents of the now abandoned village of Erisco; it is now a haven for seabirds and otters. The furthest point of the headland is the best place on Skye to watch minke whales, attracted here in summer for the rich plankton and small fish at the meeting of tidal currents.

Once back on the clifftops, the path heads around the wide sweep of Duntulm Bay, passing below Erisco and with views ahead to Duntulm Castle – a magical place at sunset. Eventually the walk passes the cottages that once housed the families of the coastguards that manned the lookout, before returning to the start along a minor road.

RUBHA HUNISH

DISTANCE: 8.4KM/5.2 MILES » **TOTAL ASCENT**: 304M/997FT » **START GR**: NG 423743 » **TIME**: ALLOW 4 HOURS **MAP**: OS EXPLORER 408, SKYE: TROTTERNISH & THE STORR, 1:25,000 » **REFRESHMENTS**: UIG HOTEL, UIG; COLUMBA 1400, STAFFIN » **NAVIGATION**: MAINLY STRAIGHTFORWARD; PATH DOWN TO HEADLAND INVOLVES MINOR SCRAMBLING.

Directions – Rubha Hunish

S→ There is a small car park just off the A855 (next to the telephone box at the Shulista turning) near Kilmaluag. From the car park, **cross the cattle grid and turn left** on to a path. **Keep on the path**, which can be wet in places, as it keeps to slightly higher ground to cross the heather moorland. The ruins of the village of Erisco can be seen to the left with the sea beyond. Eventually **go through a kissing gate** in a fence.

2 Shortly after the fence **keep right at a fork** to climb up on to the higher ground of Meall Tuath on a smaller path. Keep on the path and **aim for the whitewashed building** as it comes into view ahead. This former coastguard lookout is now an open shelter for walkers maintained by volunteers from the Mountain Bothies Association. It makes the perfect place to take shelter and enjoy the views over the sea. On a clear day the mountains of the Outer Hebrides can clearly be made out and with binoculars you may spot passing marine mammals as well as ships.

3 From the bothy **follow a rough path heading south-west** that soon descends into the depression between Meall Deas and neighbouring Meall Tuath. Once down in the dip **bear right** towards the sea. **Climb two stiles** on the left then reach a gate next to a large boulder near the cliff edge.

4 **Turn right to go through the gate. Descend a rocky staircase** where you may need to use your hands; being in a groove relieves much of the sense of exposure. After the first stretch **bear right** to stay on the path as it descends to the base of the cliff and leads to a flat area of grass. **Keep straight ahead** to cross to the coast on the far side of the headland where there are some fascinatingly sculpted *geos* to explore. Reach the cliff edge.

5 At the cliff edge **turn left**, keeping the sea on your right, and make your way around the headland. This is an excellent place to spot otters in the water, great skuas, gannets and sometimes puffins and, from the northernmost point, minke whales and other cetaceans.

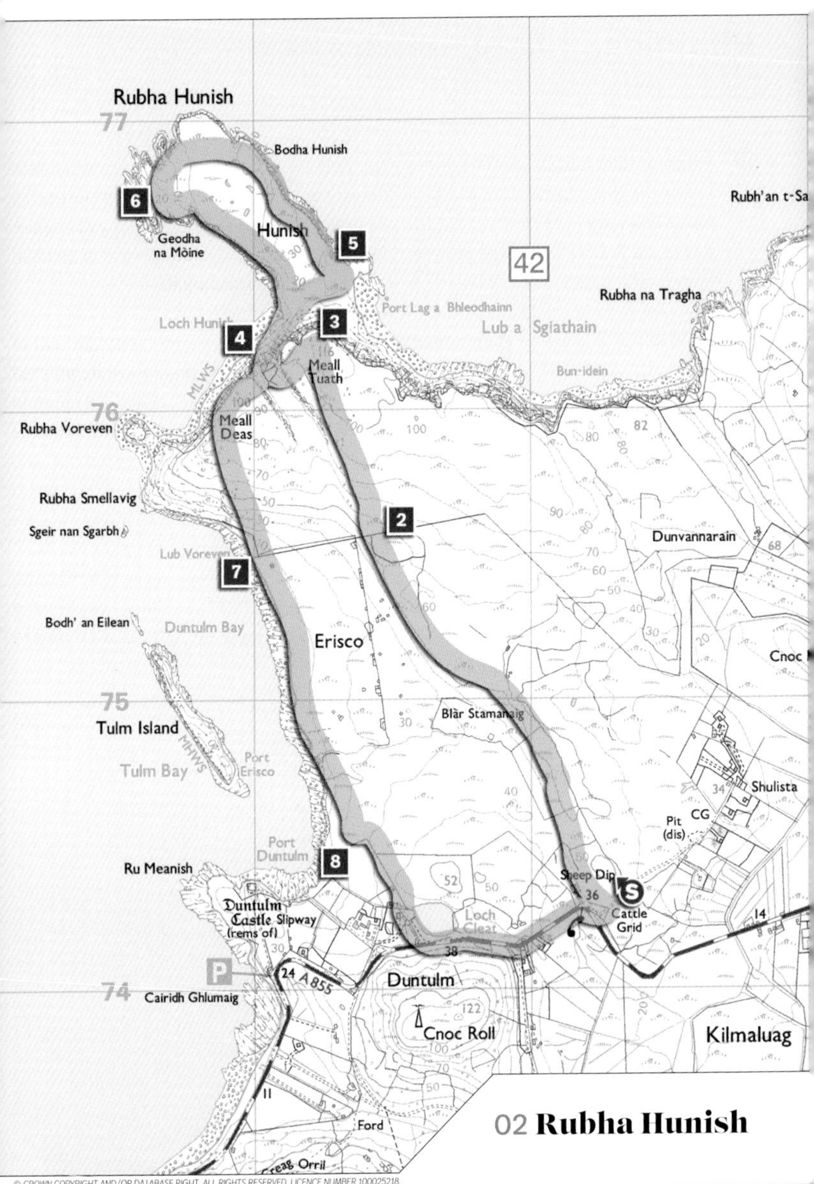

02 **Rubha Hunish**

Directions – Rubha Hunish continued ...

6 **Follow a faint path** around the west side of Rubha Hunish and eventually **bear right** under the cliffs to pick up the path leading back up to the top. **Climb the rocky scramble path** and go through the gate at the top. **Turn right** on to a vague path which leads uphill on to Meall Deas; there are great views down on to the Hunish. Stay on the path which curves to the south and **descend to a gate**.

7 Go through the gate and **keep heading straight ahead**, keeping the sea over to your right. This is a good place to watch seals in the water and sometimes otters. The island just offshore is Tulm Island and beyond it the clifftop ruins of Duntulm Castle can be seen. To the left, the ruins of the abandoned houses of the crofting village of Erisco overlook the sea.

8 Eventually **bear left to follow a drystone wall** uphill and round a corner. **Go through a gate** in a fence and keep the wall on your right until a gate on the right is reached. **Turn right through the gate** and **bear left** on a track towards a group of houses. These were the coastguard cottages which once housed the families of the men who manned the lookout on the headland. **Follow the track** up to the main road and **turn left**. After 1km **turn left** at the telephone box to return to the start.

LOOKING BACK TO THE LOOKOUT ATOP THE CLIFFS

VIEW DOWN TO THE HUNISH PENINSULA

LOOKING DOWN OVER THE BIZARRE LANDSCAPE OF THE QUIRAING

03 Quiraing

6.3km/3.9 miles

Explore one of Scotland's most iconic landscapes, where an ancient landslip from the Trotternish Ridge has formed a mass of bizarre pinnacles and crags.

Staffin to Uig road » gully scramble » The Prison » The Needle » Flodigarry path junction » Fir Bhreugach » cliffs above The Table » Maoladh Mòr » Staffin to Uig road

Start

Car park above hairpins on the Staffin to Uig road. GR: NG 440679.

The Walk

The bizarre landscape of the Quiraing is one of the most photographed in Scotland. Most visitors venture only a short distance along the base, but this circuit over the summit provides an unforgettable outing. There is parking at the top of the minor road from Staffin to Uig, 3 kilometres west from the turn off at Brogaig. The drama of the landscape is immediately apparent, with the escarpment of the Trotternish Ridge providing high cliffs in both directions. This is a landform that is still evolving, very gradually slipping towards the sea over millions of years.

The walk itself heads directly towards the pinnacles and crags that make up the Quiraing (pronounced 'kwe-rang'; *A' Chuith-Raing* in Gaelic). The path is easy to follow and after an initial flat section a minor obstacle in the form of a rocky gully needs to be overcome. This is easy enough with care, but can be slippery in wet weather. The route then heads on to pass between the two of the best-known rock features, The Prison – a castle-like rocky outcrop over to your right – and The Needle – a pinnacle up the slope to your left.

Here the walk becomes rougher underfoot. Continue below the cliffs and among the rock features of the Quiraing; the route eventually climbs up to the escarpment before heading back along the clifftop for sensational views down over the Quiraing, the crofting township of Staffin, the sea and the mainland beyond. Immediately below is a raised, flat, grassy platform known as The Table; you may see figures on it who have climbed up to it from below, but it's much better seen from above. The descent back down to the start is steep and can be slippery in wet weather, but completes a classic circuit.

QUIRAING

DISTANCE: 6.3KM/3.9 MILES » **TOTAL ASCENT**: 495M/1,624FT » **START GR**: NG 440679 » **TIME**: ALLOW 3.5 HOURS » **MAP**: OS EXPLORER 408, SKYE: TROTTERNISH & THE STORR, 1:25,000 » **REFRESHMENTS**: COLUMBA 1400, STAFFIN; UIG HOTEL, UIG » **NAVIGATION**: CLEAR PATH INITIALLY; CAREFUL NAVIGATION NEEDED ON HILL SECTION ESPECIALLY IN POOR VISIBILITY. SMALL SCRAMBLE, HIGH CLIFFS AND STEEP DESCENT.

Directions - Quiraing

S Park in the car park at the summit of the minor road linking Staffin and Uig; there is room for a good number of cars, but it can get busy. If full, there is more space further west along the road towards Uig - do not park on the hairpin bends or in any of the passing places. To start, **follow the path signed *Flodigarry*** on the opposite side of the road from the car park. There are great views down over the crofts, houses and bay at Staffin, and also along the Trotternish Ridge in both directions. Stay on the clear path eventually reaching a rocky gully.

2 **Cross this gully** with care using the rocky steps and continue ahead, climbing gently. A path on the right detours to The Prison, a large outcrop with three summits which looks like a fortress. (Ascending to The Prison is via a scramble on loose rock and isn't recommended.) **Stay on the main path** to climb up loose gravel, or scree, keeping The Prison on your right. To the left is the main area of the Quiraing, where huge sections of rock have detached themselves from the high cliffs behind leaving an atmospheric jumble of pinnacles and crags to explore. Up on the left is The Needle, an impressive 37m pinnacle. Above The Needle is The Table and it is possible to detour up to it by following a faint rocky path on the left, but it is very steep and eroded with a lot of loose rock underfoot; it's much better seen from above later in the walk.

3 **Continue on the main path** and cross a slope to **pass under an overhang**. The path rounds a bend, and a smaller set of towers and crags comes into view. **Climb a stile** over a fence and continue on the path ahead. **Fork left** at a path junction (the path on the right descends to Loch Hasco and on to Flodigarry). The path now leads up to a saddle. **Go through a gap in a stone wall** and stay on the path, passing smaller pinnacles. **Climb more steeply** as the path ascends the slope on the left - here it follows a deep, eroded groove as it climbs to the ridge.

4 **Climb a stile** and emerge on to the ridgeline with amazing views all round and the prow of Sròn Vourlinn to the right. **Turn left** and follow the cliff edge uphill, staying a safe distance from the edge. **Climb steadily**; further on there are views down to the grassy, flat surface of The Table, where it is said locals once hid their cattle out of sight from Viking raiders.

5 **Continue to the highest point of the cliff**, set away from the moorland summit of Meall na Suiramach. The mass of pinnacles and crags can really be appreciated from this bird's-eye viewpoint. On a clear day, the Torridon Hills can be seen across the sea with Staffin Island in the foreground. **Follow the path** as it starts to head downhill, aiming across the slope to reach a gate in a fence. **Go through the gate** and head more directly downhill. This is very eroded, steep and boggy in places, so care is needed. Eventually **turn right** on to the main Quiraing path to return to the start.

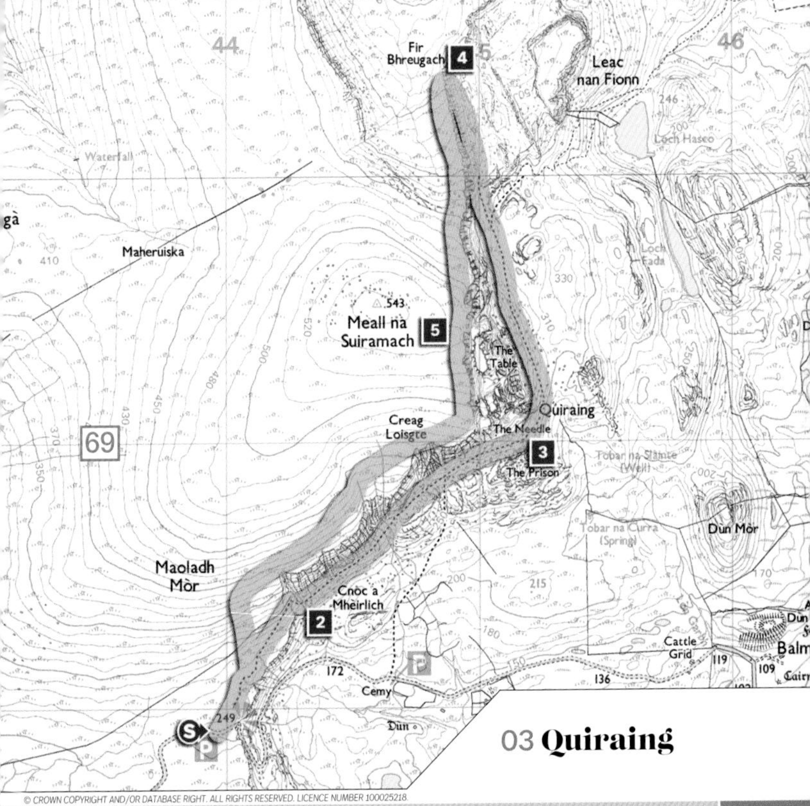

THE STORR AND ITS OLD MAN

04 The Storr & its Old Man

7.9km/4.9 miles

Get up close to the remarkable rock scenery around the Old Man, before leaving the crowds behind for a climb up to the summit of The Storr itself.

Old Man of Storr car park » Old Man of Storr » Coire Scamadal » The Storr » Bealach Beag » A855 » Old Man of Storr car park

Start

Old Man of Storr car park (parking charge), A855 between Portree and Staffin. GR: NG 508528.

The Walk

While the dramatic, rocky pinnacles of the Old Man and the Cathedral Rock have made the Storr Sanctuary famous, far fewer walkers venture up to the summit of The Storr itself, a remarkable viewpoint.

Starting from the large car park on the Portree to Staffin road, the walk follows a clear, wide path uphill at first; once a dense forestry plantation, these lower slopes were felled and will hopefully be replaced with native trees; there are views over the water to the islands of Rona and Raasay. The path is steep in places but easy to follow and, after a couple of gates, reaches the foot of the Old Man. This bulky 50-metre pillar was climbed by Don Whillans in the 1950s who described the loose rock as 'like climbing porridge'. It's just part of a remarkable assemblage of rock formations known as the Sanctuary; the walk then passes below another, the Cathedral Rock, pierced by two holes.

Leaving most visitors behind, the walk heads north and, after a slight scramble, traverses a high path on a wide arc around Coire Scamadal, with views north to Staffin Bay and along the ridge towards the Quiraing. Careful navigation is needed to find the point to leave the main path for the climb up to the summit of The Storr, a truly fantastic vantage point.

After leaving the summit the walk follows the cliff edge and provides aerial views down over the Sanctuary and the Old Man. The descent is grassy underfoot at first, but later heads down a steep, rocky gully to leave the ridge. The walk ends with a final grassy amble back down to the road.

THE STORR & ITS OLD MAN

DISTANCE: 7.9KM/4.9 MILES » **TOTAL ASCENT**: 613M/2,011FT » **START GR**: NG 508528 » **TIME**: ALLOW 5 HOURS » **MAP**: OS EXPLORER 408, SKYE: TROTTERNISH & THE STORR, 1:25,000 » **REFRESHMENTS**: STORR VIEW COFFEE, NEAR OLD MAN OF STORR CAR PARK; COLUMBA 1400, STAFFIN » **NAVIGATION**: CAREFUL NAVIGATION NEEDED AT COIRE SCAMADAL; DESCENT PATH IS STEEP AND ROCKY.

Directions – The Storr & its Old Man

S The walk begins from the top end of the Old Man of Storr car park. Follow the path and **climb uphill**. The visible tree stumps are a reminder of the dense commercial forestry plantation which once clothed these lower slopes. Now that they have been felled, native woodland is being encouraged and there are also great views back over to the offshore islands of Rona and Raasay and also to Applecross on the Scottish mainland.

2 **Continue uphill, passing through two gates** to reach the open grazing moorland with the vast cliffs of The Storr visible ahead. The area in front of the high cliffs is known as the Sanctuary and includes the huge pinnacle of the Old Man itself. **Stay on the main path** which heads uphill towards the base of the Old Man. At the end of the formal path, **take the smaller path climbing diagonally to the right**. Pass below the Cathedral Rock which has two large 'window' holes piercing it. **Keep along a fainter path** to climb between a small craggy knoll on the right and the main cliffs on the left to reach a col.

3 From the col, a short detour to the right up the knoll provides a picture-perfect view of the Old Man backed by the Storr Lochs. Back at the col, **climb the stile** over the fence and **bear left to stay on the path**. The path is narrow but clear, with good views north along the Trotternish Ridge. **Keep left at a fork** to get to a very short, rocky scramble up a rock step (the right-hand path has a similar obstacle but feels more exposed). **Climb up over the rock step** and continue along the path as it contours around Coire Scamadal.

4 The route turns off the main path approximately 1km after the rocky step and the correct point can be hard to find. Look out for when the grassy slopes up to your left have become clear of rocks; at this point there's a tiny cairn. **Turn sharp left up an indistinct path** to reach the broad ridge of The Storr, where the path peters out. **Keep left along the ridge** and eventually up to the trig point which marks the summit of The Storr.

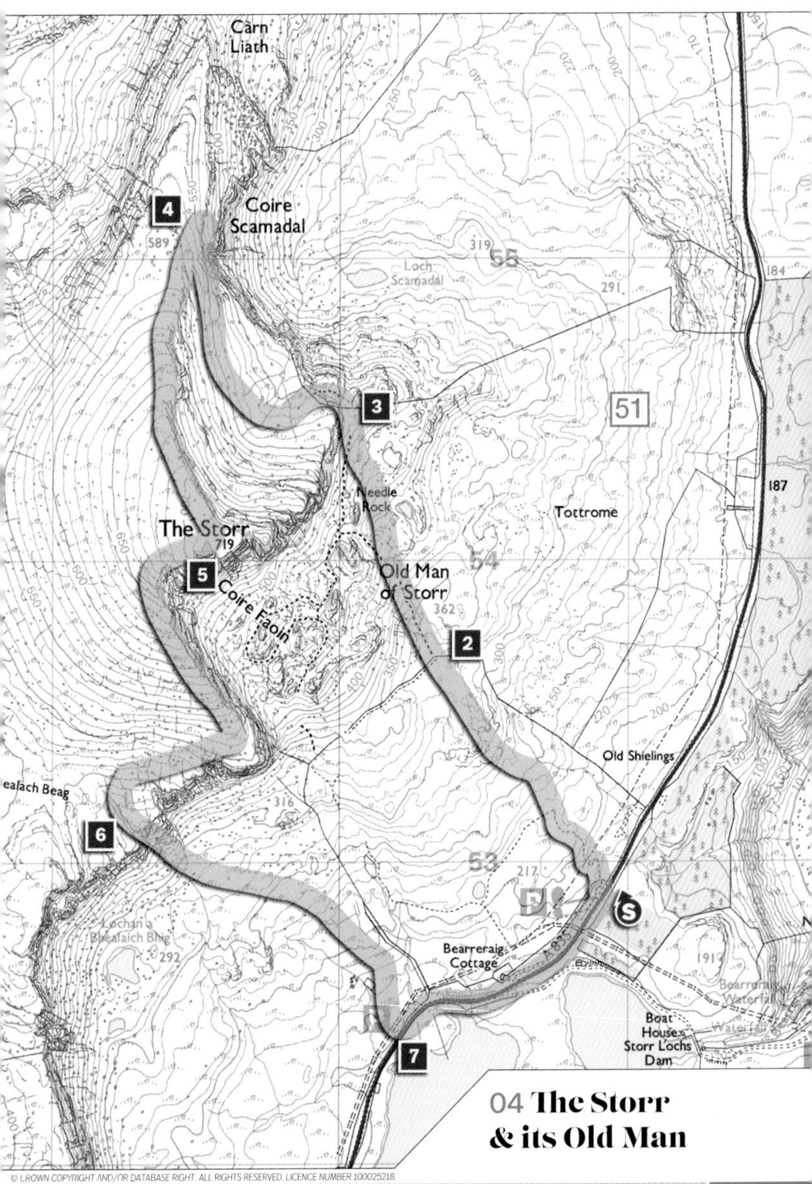

04 The Storr & its Old Man

Directions - The Storr & its Old Man continued ...

5 At 719m this is the highest point on the Trotternish Ridge and provides superb all-round views as far as the Outer Hebrides and the mountains on the mainland as well as the Cuillin Hills and the flat-topped MacLeod's Tables to the west. Now **follow the cliff edge**, keeping well away from the huge drops on your left. Skirt a deep scree gully and **continue gently downhill**, following the line of the escarpment. Very soon wonderful views open up of the Sanctuary and the pinnacles far below. Follow the top of the cliffs as they bear right and continue downhill; the path is indistinct in places. Once down on the flatter ground **continue ahead until you reach the top of a gully** with a stream running into it.

6 Make sure you are in the correct place as it is not possible to safely descend anywhere else. **Take the path on the left-hand side of the stream**, which quickly descends very steeply over rocky terrain. While the path is rough it is clear to follow; keep close to the left-hand side of the water. When the grassy ground is reached below the cliffs, **continue ahead** on a worn path across open grazing ground. **Keep straight ahead** to cross a faint quad track and then **bear half left** to head nearer to a fence marking the edge of the felled area at the base of The Storr. Keep working your way downhill and when the road comes into view **bear slightly right to aim for a metal farm gate**.

7 Go through the gate, **cross the road and turn left**. Follow a path on the verge for around 800m to return to the start.

THE OLD MAN

Section 2

North-West Skye

Skye's farthest flung peninsula is Duirinish in the north-west. It has one of the most dramatic sections of coastline in all Britain. While Neist Point has become a popular spot on the tourist trail, most of the rest of the great cliffs here – towering to over 300 metres in places – are little known or visited.

Inland from the cliffs is a wild moorland where the strange flat-topped MacLeod's Tables dominate the landscape. Dunvegan, famed for its castle, is the gateway to the area, while Glendale – now community owned – is the main settlement on the peninsula itself.

RAMASAIG CLIFF

MACLEOD'S MAIDENS

DESCENT TO RAMASAIG BAY

05 The Hoe & Waterstein Head 14.9km/9.3 miles

Three distinct clifftop summits provide fabulous views on this coastal circuit that returns via a quiet minor road, where sheep far outnumber vehicles.

Ramasaig » Lorgill track » The Hoe » Hoe Rape » Ramasaig Bay » Ramasaig Cliff » Waterstein Head » Beinn na Còinnich track » Ramasaig

Start

Ramasaig road end (roadside parking). Take the minor road from the B884 after Glendale. GR: NG 164443.

The Walk

Starting among the cattle and sheep of a remote croft to the west of Dunvegan, the walk leaves a muddy track after two kilometres to cross boggy moorland heading towards the sea. A rough climb leads to the impressive high cliffs of The Hoe and the first views along this wild and spectacular section of Skye's coast.

The going along the rim of the cliffs from here is on springy turf with few navigational demands apart from keeping the sea and steep cliffs on your left. A straightforward descent leads past a stunning headland en route to Ramasaig Bay, before the steady climb up to Ramasaig Cliff. The cliffs are draped with waterfalls as the route descends again, with a stunning section of cliffs at Moonen Bay.

The final ascent of this roller-coaster route is up the grassy slopes to Waterstein Head, offering the finest views of the day; even the famed cliffs of Neist Point look tiny from up here. Rest against the summit trig point atop this near-vertical cliff and keep an eye out for the white-tailed eagles. Reintroduced to the west coast of Scotland in the mid-1970s, these majestic birds are sometimes seen riding the thermals here.

The return route follows a vague track back to the quiet Ramasaig road; you may have to squeeze past the sheep, who seek it out for warmth and salt.

THE HOE & WATERSTEIN HEAD

DISTANCE: 14.9KM/9.3 MILES » **TOTAL ASCENT**: 1,109M/3,638M » **START GR**: NG 164443 » **TIME**: ALLOW 6 HOURS **MAP**: OS EXPLORER 407, SKYE: DUNVEGAN, 1:25,000 » **REFRESHMENTS**: THE DUNVEGAN DELI-CAFE OR BLAS CAFE, DUNVEGAN » **NAVIGATION**: STRAIGHTFORWARD IN GOOD WEATHER; CARE NEEDED NEAR HIGH CLIFFS.

Directions – The Hoe & Waterstein Head

S Take the rough minor road to Ramasaig; there is limited parking near a cottage at the road end or further back in an old quarry where the route returns to the road near the end of the walk. Don't block any passing places, turning areas or gates. **Follow the road** past the cottage, heading slightly downhill. **Continue on to a track**, passing farm buildings and crossing a stream; **go straight on through a gate** and out on to the open moor. Cattle and sheep graze here, and it can often be very muddy.

2 After 2km, just before a gate and before the track descends to Lorgill, **turn right** towards the coast and the cliffs of The Hoe. **Cross pathless, boggy terrain**, following faint quad tracks in places, **aiming left** of the highest ground on a rising traverse and keeping any rocky crags on your left. This tricky section ends at the steep cliffs of The Hoe, with spectacular views to the MacLeod's Maidens sea stacks away to the south and the Cuillin Hills beyond visible on a clear day.

3 **Bear right** to walk away from this view; **follow a faint path** along the clifftop with the sea on your left. **Descend gradually** to reach the promontory of Hoe Rape, a good place from which to spot passing porpoises, seals and whales; in the summer months you might even spot a basking shark. **Descend the grassy clifftops** to reach the back of Ramasaig Bay and **cross a burn**. **Go through a gate** in the fence ahead and turn left. Stay on the landward side of the fence and reach a second burn.

4 **Cross the burn and climb steeply**, keeping near the fence until the summit of Ramasaig Cliff is reached. Here the sharp pull up is rewarded by spectacular views north of the great cliffs of Waterstein Head and across Moonen Bay to the headland lighthouse at Neist Point. **Descend**, still on the landward side of the fence, and detour slightly inland to **cross the Moonen Burn**. **Climb steadily** up grassy slopes to reach the highest point on the walk, Waterstein Head.

5 Waterstein Head is marked by a trig point and offers precipitous views down to the breaking waves 296m below. From the trig point **head back** the way you came for 500m. Here **bear east-south-east** and follow a faint, grassy track to the col before Beinn na Còinnich. **Go through a gate** and keep to the left of the hill, continuing to eventually reach the Ramasaig road at its high point. **Turn right** to return to the start.

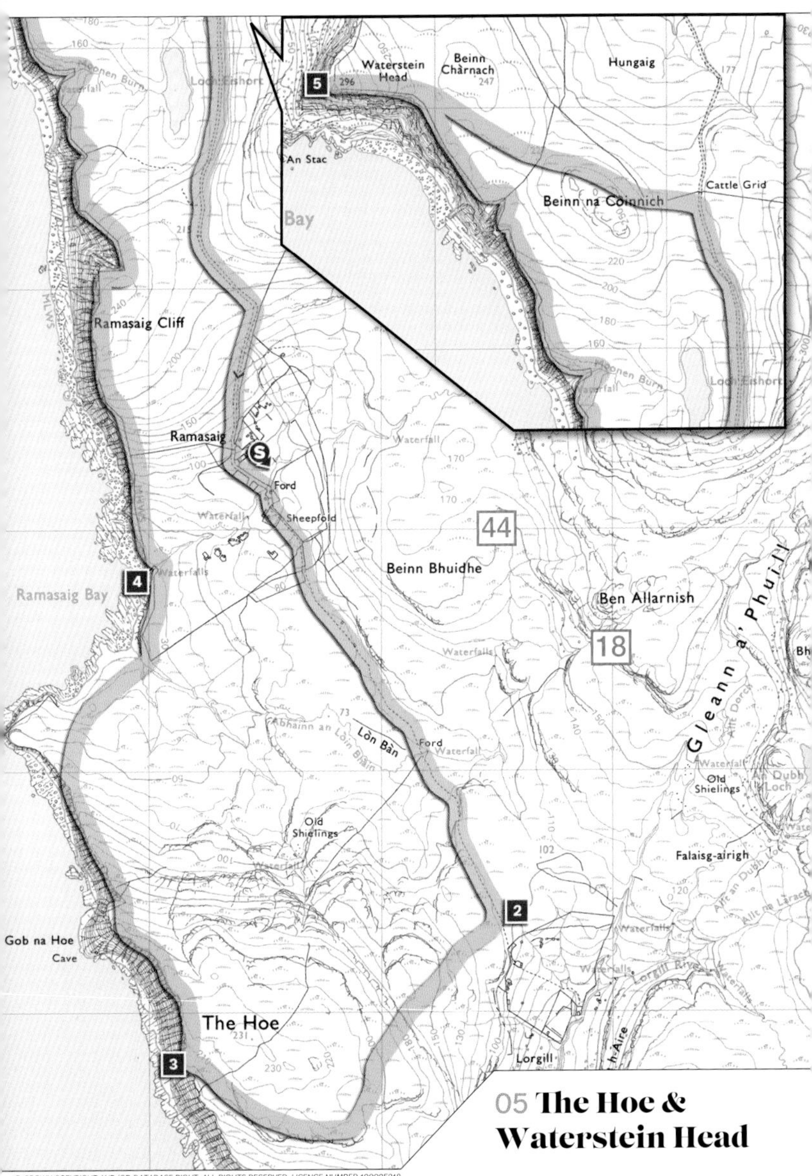

05 The Hoe & Waterstein Head

CLIFFS ON THE APPROACH TO THE MAIDENS

06 Ramasaig to Orbost via MacLeod's Maidens

22.9km/14.2 miles

A challenging linear coastal walk above some of Britain's wildest and most spectacular cliffs, passing the remains of cleared settlements.

Ramasaig » Lorgill River » Glen Dibidal » Glen Ollisdal » Glen Lorgasdal » MacLeod's Maidens » Idrigill » Brandarsaig » Orbost

Start

Ramasaig road end (roadside parking). Take the minor road from the B884 after Glendale. GR: NG 164443.

Finish

Car park near Orbost House. GR: NG 257431.

The Walk

This linear walk is both strenuous and remote; it should not be underestimated. It does require transport to be arranged, but it's worth it to experience the most spectacular clifftop scenery on Skye. The route passes close Ollisdal Bothy, so with the right gear could become a two-day mini adventure.

Initially following a track from the isolated croft at Ramasaig, the route reaches Lorgill, where a wade of the burn may be necessary. Lorgill was once home to around 12 households, but in 1830 they were ordered to pack and board ships bound for Canada. Such orders were commonplace during the Highland Clearances. The route then hugs the coast on pathless, rough ground, crossing three more glens. There are constant climbs and descents, but the spectacular coastal scenery includes impressive waterfalls, sea arches, caves and stacks.

There are many reminders of previous habitation, with ruined cottages and the rippled ground where lazy beds were once fertilised by seaweed carried up from the shore in heavy creels. The final section of coast leads close to Skye's greatest sea stacks, MacLeod's Maidens, named after the wife and two daughters of a fourteenth-century clan chief who were shipwrecked and drowned here. The largest stack is the mother, said to be weaving, while the two smaller stacks are the daughters preparing the yarn. They provide a spectacular finale for the west coast; the walk then heads inland on the final section through woodland, eventually reaching a track which leads to Orbost.

RAMASAIG TO ORBOST VIA MACLEOD'S MAIDENS

DISTANCE: 22.9KM/14.2 MILES » **TOTAL ASCENT**: 1,119M/3,671M » **START GR**: NG 164443 » **TIME**: ALLOW 10 HOURS
MAP: OS EXPLORER 407, SKYE: DUNVEGAN, 1:25,000 » **REFRESHMENTS**: THE DUNVEGAN DELI-CAFE OR BLAS CAFE, DUNVEGAN » **NAVIGATION**: GOOD MAP READING SKILLS NEEDED ESPECIALLY IN POOR WEATHER; TAKE CARE NEAR HIGH CLIFFS.

Directions – Ramasaig to Orbost via MacLeod's Maidens

S Take the rough minor road to Ramasaig; there is limited parking near a cottage at the road end. Don't block any passing places, turning areas or gates. Take the road **slightly downhill** and **continue on to the track** past a large barn. **Cross the stream** and **go through a gate** near the last farm buildings and out on to the open moorland. Cattle and sheep graze here, and it can be extremely muddy after wet weather. After 2km **go through a gate** and **head downhill** to reach the ruins of the settlement of Lorgill.

2 **Cross the Lorgill River** (if it's too deep here, it may be easier to cross at the beach). On the far side, **turn right** and pass more ruins to reach the sea. **Bear left** to climb a faint coastal path to the top of the Biod Boidheach cliff.

3 **Follow the clifftop** until a deep inlet or *geo* makes it necessary to **detour inland**; there is a great view of a sea arch here. **Head back to the coast and keep left** for a lovely section of dramatic cliffs, a couple of coves, and better going underfoot. Look out for a sea cave that pierces right through the cliff, allowing a dramatic paddle for kayakers. The three sea stacks known as MacLeod's Maidens can be seen in the distance. After the third cove, **pick up a faint track** and follow it down to the Geodha Mòr.

4 At the back of the inlet **cross the Dibidal River** at the ford. **Turn right** to reach the coast and resume the clifftop route, climbing at first and then descending into Glen Ollisdal (Ollisdal Bothy is around 1km inland from here). **Cross the burn** and continue along the coastline for a spectacular section taking in impressive sea stacks, waterfalls and natural arches. **Follow an indistinct path uphill** to An Dainnire, the finest section, with stunning views in both directions.

LOOKING BACK ALONG THE CLIFFTOPS

CONTINUES ON PAGE 36

06 Ramasaig to Orbost via MacLeod's Maidens

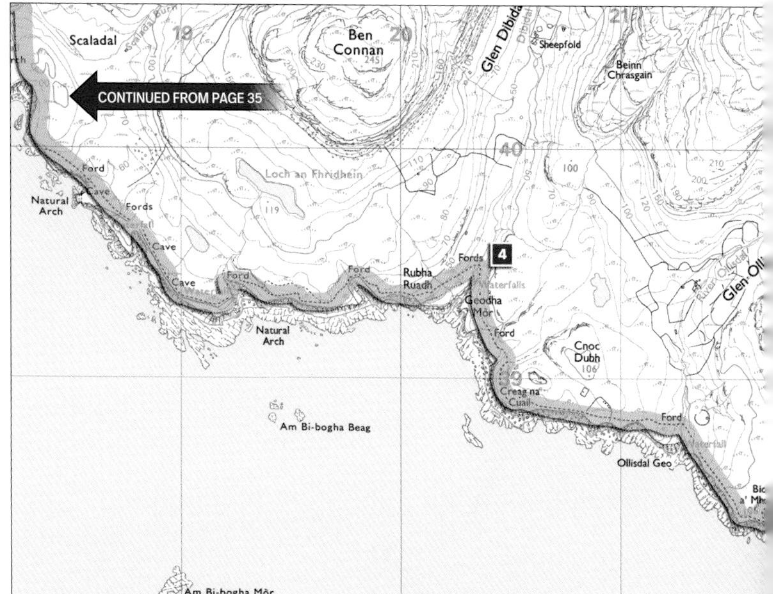

5 Eventually **descend on narrow sheep tracks and cross the burn** at the back of Inghir a' Ghàrraidh. Follow the coast as the cliff descends to reach the headland overlooking MacLeod's Maidens, three sea stacks comprising the 70m-high mother and two much shorter daughters. **Continue along the cliff** for a short distance then **bear left to head inland**, aiming just to the right of a steep slope to reach the Glac Ghealaridh valley. **Cross the slopes** on the far side as the path becomes easier to follow. Soon reach the ruins of the village of Idrigill, once home to around 15 households before the Highland Clearances.

6 **Follow the path** past the ruins and head into the trees. **Stay on the path** as it undulates through a mixture of fir plantation and woodland including Rebel's Wood, planted in memory of Joe Strummer, lead singer of The Clash, whose grandmother came from the Isle of Raasay.

7 **Continue past the clearing** at Brandarsaig and head uphill. **After 2km pick up a forestry track** which leads down to the shore at the head of Loch Bharcasaig. At the back of the bay **turn left** and stay on the track as it leads inland to reach Orbost House and the car park at the end of the walk.

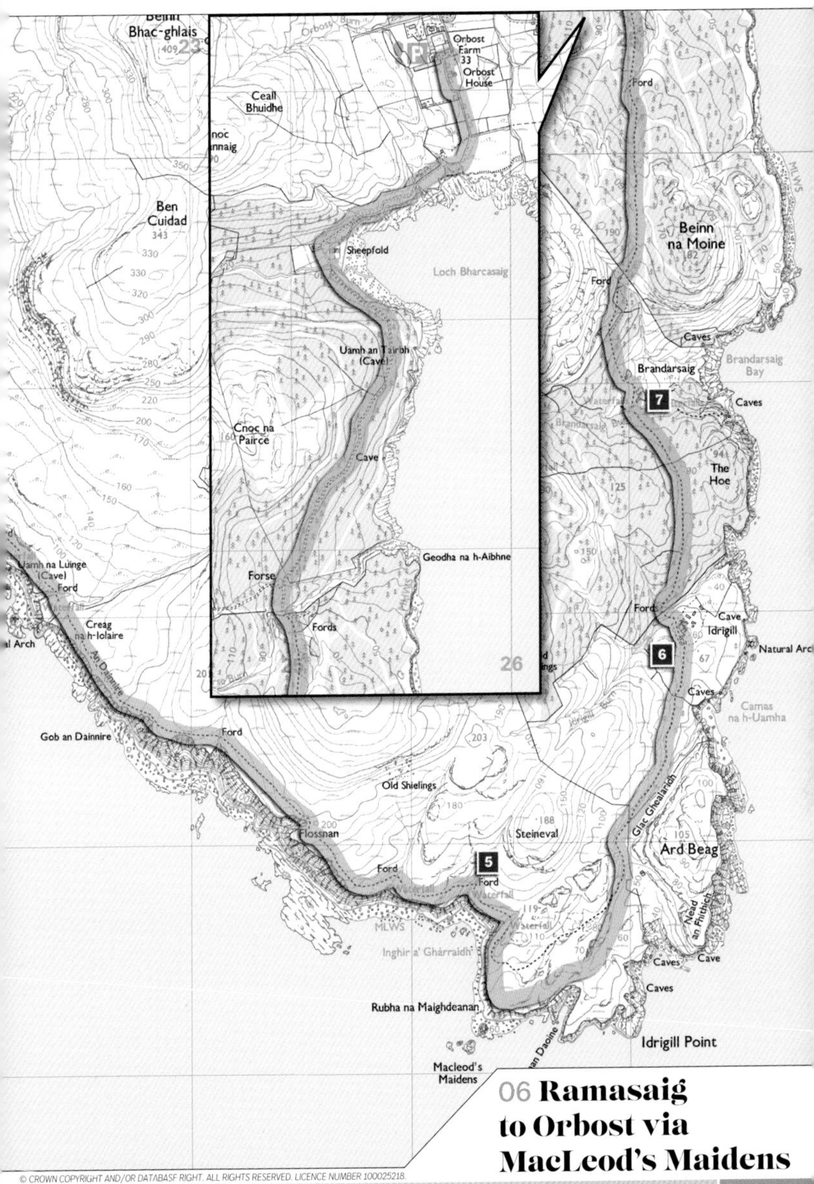

06 Ramasaig to Orbost via MacLeod's Maidens

Section 3

Glen Brittle & Sligachan

The Black Cuillin are the most spectacular and challenging mountains in Britain. These are peaks of which many hillwalkers' dreams are made – and their nightmares! Some of their peaks require scrambling or even rock climbing to reach; the summits described here are among the more accessible, but are still far rockier and more rugged than mainland mountains.

Adjacent to the Cuillin, as seen in the view from Sligachan, are the Red Hills – their steep and shapely flanks covered in extensive screes. Although lacking the great cliffs and exposure of their near neighbours, they can match them for views and for strenuous ascents. Across Glen Brittle are extensive forestry plantations that make for easier walking, while the Rubha an Dùnain peninsula offers a fascinating journey into the past.

CLACH GLAS SEEN FROM MARSCO

COLLIE AND MACKENZIE, BACKED BY MARSCO

LOOKING BACK FROM CREAG MHÒR

07 Rubha an Dùnain 13.7km/8.5 miles

Explore a wild coastal peninsula at the foot of the Cuillin to discover hidden treasures including a Viking canal and a Bronze Age chambered cairn.

Glenbrittle Campsite » Allt Coire Làgan crossing » Creag Mhòr » Slochd Dubh » MacAskill house ruins » Loch na h-Àirde » Rubha an Dùnain » chambered cairn » Slochd Dubh » Allt Coire Làgan crossing » Glenbrittle Campsite

Start

Car park west of Glenbrittle Campsite. Follow the minor road (turn off the B8009 east of Carbost) down Glen Brittle to the coast. GR: NG 409206.

The Walk

Early inhabitants and Norse settlers used the sea in the way we use roads today and this walk showcases some of the best-preserved remains of their handiwork on Skye. Starting from the lovely sandy beach at Glen Brittle, the walk crosses the campsite (where there is a cafe open to the public), and then heads out along the northern side of a low peninsula on a stony track.

The walk becomes much rougher once the track is left behind for a climb up a low hill. The reward is fabulous views out to sea to the distinctive islands of Eigg, Rùm and Canna, as well as back for a different perspective on the jagged Cuillin. Faint paths lead to the ruins of a once-large house, occupied until the nineteenth century by the local clan chief.

More ancient remains can be seen once the wet moorland is crossed to reach Loch na h-Àirde. Here Viking settlers created a canal to provide access to the loch, which it is thought they used as an early shipyard; some impressive Norse artefacts have been discovered here. Nearby, the walls of an Iron Age fort overlook the sea, giving Rubha an Dùnain its name, which translates as the headland of the fort.

A rough walk, often pathless, leads to the headland itself, a great place to soak up the views and wildlife on a clear day. From here the route turns back alongside Loch Brittle passing an impressive chambered cairn dating from the Bronze Age. The inner walls of this ancient burial chamber remain intact. The final stretch of the walk retraces the outward route, now with the mighty Cuillin ahead; finish with a rest on the beach at Glen Brittle.

RUBHA AN DÙNAIN

DISTANCE: 13.7KM/8.5 MILES » **TOTAL ASCENT**: 350M/1,148FT » **START GR**: NG 409206 » **TIME**: ALLOW 6 HOURS
MAP: OS EXPLORER 411, SKYE: CUILLIN HILLS, 1:25,000 » **REFRESHMENTS**: GLENBRITTLE CAMPSITE CAFE
NAVIGATION: STRAIGHTFORWARD, ALTHOUGH NOT WAYMARKED AND OVER ROUGH GROUND.

Directions – Rubha an Dùnain

S Glenbrittle Campsite occupies an enviable position behind the sandy beach at the foot of the glen. **Begin from the parking area** just before the campsite (you can pay to park in the campsite itself if the car park is full). **Walk through the campsite** and on to a path to the left of the toilet block to reach a stony track. **Turn right** to follow the track which runs above Loch Brittle, soon crossing a small burn.

2 **After 2km cross the Allt Coire Làgan**. There is a bridge a short way to the right if the water level is high. **Continue along the track**, crossing another minor burn with a waterfall after 1.5km. **Fork left** on a clear path to climb towards the low hill of Creag Mhòr.

3 From the summit of Creag Mhòr there are great views out to the Small Isles of Eigg, Rùm and Canna. **Keep straight ahead** over the final high point, ignoring a faint path to the left, and then **descend steeply** on a rough and indistinct path into a dip. Cutting across the peninsula, this is known as the Slochd Dubh, or black ditch. From here, **pick up a grassy track** which follows on from the stony track coming from the right. **Go left** on the track and **pass through a gap in a stone wall**. Follow the grassy track as it runs alongside the wall and then **aim right (south-west)** to cross boggy ground, with high bracken and then bogs; the path fades out. **Aim for the ruins** of a large house, once home to the Clan MacAskill chief.

THE DUN, FROM BEYOND LOCH NA H-ÀIRDE

Bualintur
Ford
Cuillin Cottage
Boat House
Fords
Culnamean
An Dùnan
FB
Fords
Mussel Scalp
MLWS
Sgùrr Bhreatail
Waterfall
Fords
Buaile Dhubh
Ford
Loch Brittle
Lochan Coir' a' Ghobhainn
Coir' a' Ghobhain
Cave
Rubha na Creige Mòire
Creag Mhòr
Càrn Mòr
Sloc hd Dubh
Sgùrr nan Cearcall
Stachd
Camas a' Mhùrain
Chambered Cairn
Cairn
Rubha an Dùnain
Loch na h-Àirde
Cave
Creag a' Chapaill
Dun
Sgeir Mhòr
07 Rubha an Dùnain

Directions - Rubha an Dùnain continued ...

4 From the ruins, **bear right** and keep to the edge of a low escarpment to avoid the worst bog. **Keep straight ahead (west-south-west)** to reach Loch na h-Àirde, halfway along its near shore. **Turn left** to cross the rough and sodden ground near the loch to reach the outflow. It is thought that this channel was actually constructed by the Vikings who may have used the loch as a place to mend their boats. (You can detour up to the low hill on the left to explore the remains of an ancient fort, or dun, overlooking the sea; it probably dates back to the Iron Age.)

5 **Cross the channel** (it is usually possible on stepping stones; do not attempt if the water levels are very high). **Pass a small stone shelter** and from there **climb up a low cliff**. Now **follow the coast** on mainly pathless ground to reach the westernmost point of the headland - a good place to admire the views and watch for whales and dolphins. **Keep the sea on your left** as you continue round the headland and eventually **descend to a wall** that leads from the coast to Loch na h-Àirde.

6 **Go through the gap** in the wall and turn right. Soon the remains of one of the best preserved of Skye's Bronze Age chambered cairns is reached. It is possible to crawl through the entrance to enter the inner chamber, used to bury the dead around 4,000 years ago. **Aim left (north)** to return to the northern shore of the peninsula. **Keep on a faint path** between the sea and some crags and then descend to the Slochd Dubh. **Pick up the stony track** and follow this back - retracing the outward route - to the campsite and the start.

DISTANT SGÙRR ALASDAIR

THE CUILLIN RIDGE FROM ACROSS GLEN BRITTLE

08 Bealach Brittle Loop

16km/9.9 miles

This easy-going circuit uses forestry tracks but gives views down Loch Eynort to the sea and across Glen Brittle to the majestic Cuillin.

Fairy Pools car park » track junction » Braigh Brunal » Coire Mòr » Bealach Brittle » Fairy Pools car park

Start

Fairy Pools car park, Glen Brittle (parking charge). Follow the minor road (turn off the B8009 east of Carbost) down Glen Brittle; the car park is on the right-hand side after the first descent into the glen. GR: NG 424258.

The Walk

Glen Brittle curves around the western side of the Cuillin, before leading down to the sea at a sandy beach. This walk loops around the opposite side of the glen, using easy forestry tracks for a variety of excellent views. The route is usually very quiet, in contrast to the busy Fairy Pools across the other side of the road.

From a gate at the top end of the car park a forestry track leads gently uphill and the Cuillin views are left behind for a climb up through the trees. The track runs high above Glen Eynort, overlooking the fields and sea loch beyond. A couple of picnic tables offer a good chance for a rest and to enjoy views over the trees to the sea and the distant Outer Hebrides.

After a fairly flat section, the route climbs steadily to eventually reach Bealach Brittle, the pass between Glen Eynort and Glen Brittle. Suddenly the views become much more dramatic, with the Cuillin Ridge seen at full stature towering across the glen, a huge wall of cliffs and scree.

The final section has magnificent views into the Cuillin coires; the Inaccessible Pinnacle on the top of Sgùrr Dearg is one of many summits you can pick out. As the track heads back to the car park, the well-worn route down to the Fairy Pools is visible on the far side of the road. This series of crystal-clear pools linked by waterfalls and an underground arch have become extremely popular in recent years. Even if busy, they are still worth a short detour at the end.

BEALACH BRITTLE LOOP

DISTANCE: 16KM/9.9 MILES » **TOTAL ASCENT**: 506M/1,660FT » **START GR**: NG 424258 » **TIME**: ALLOW 4.5 HOURS **MAP**: OS EXPLORER 411, SKYE: CUILLIN HILLS, 1:25,000 » **REFRESHMENTS**: GLENBRITTLE CAMPSITE CAFE OR TAIGH AILEAN HOTEL, PORTNALONG » **NAVIGATION**: STRAIGHTFORWARD.

FOREST TRACK

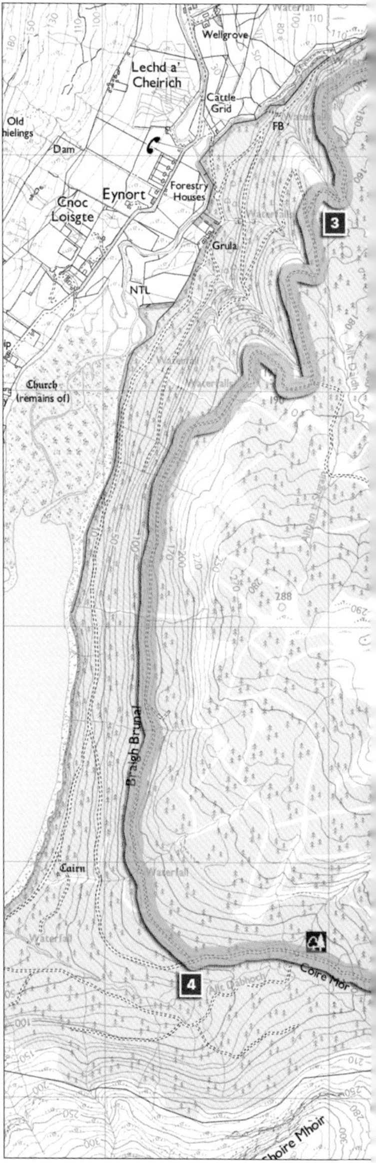

08 **Bealach Brittle Loop**

Directions – Bealach Brittle Loop

S **Walk to the top end of the car park** and **go through the gate** on to a forestry track. The walk is waymarked in yellow. **Turn right** at the first junction and **head uphill**, leaving the Cuillin Hills behind you.

2 After 2.2km, **turn left** at a junction to head uphill at first and then gently down. Soon there are views into Glen Eynort, where sections of the forest have been felled. The lush green glen is still farmed and includes the ruins of a medieval chapel possibly founded by St Maelrubha, a monk who with his followers spread Christianity throughout the west coast of Scotland after leaving Ireland in AD 671. The track now runs high above Loch Eynort.

3 **Turn left** at the next junction (the branch to the right descends to Eynort). **Continue along the track** as it bends first right and then left. **Turn right** at the next junction. There are good views out over the sea to the Outer Hebrides. Keep an eye out for white-tailed eagles that sometimes fish here. Pass a couple of picnic tables; the second has the better views. Descend gently to reach a junction.

4 **Turn left**, following the yellow waymarkers. Stay on the track to **cross a bridge and keep left**, ignoring a track to the right. **Climb steadily** to eventually reach Bealach Brittle, the high point between the two glens. Shortly after this pass is a picnic table with views down over Loch Brittle and Rubha an Dùnain and to the Cuillin Ridge on the far side of the glen. Continue straight ahead; the track undulates across the side of the glen with great views to the Cuillin peaks opposite.

5 **Keep left at a fork** to head slightly uphill. Eventually the track returns to the first junction of the walk; **branch right** to return to the car park.

LOOKING ACROSS TO COIR' AN EICH

SGÙRR NAN GILLEAN FROM MARSCO

09 Marsco

14km/8.7 miles

With its distinctive outline and fine grassy summit ridge, Marsco avoids being overshadowed by its higher and more celebrated neighbours.

Sligachan » Glen Sligachan » Allt na Measarroch » Màm a' Phobuill » Coire nan Laogh rim » Marsco » Coire nan Laogh rim » Màm a' Phobuill » Allt na Measarroch » Glen Sligachan » Sligachan

Start

Sligachan Old Bridge car park, A87 (just east of the bridge over the River Sligachan). Additional parking available west of the bridge. GR: NG 488299.

The Walk

The grand bronze sculpture at Sligachan depicts two of the legends of Scottish mountaineering. John Mackenzie, a crofter born in nearby Sconser, began his exploration of the mountains early, summiting Sgùrr nan Gillean at the age of ten and spending his teenage summers taking Victorian guests from the Sligachan Hotel on pony trips to Loch Coruisk. Becoming the first Scottish mountain guide, he made many first ascents in the Cuillin before joining forces with Norman Collie in 1886. Collie was a privately-educated chemistry professor whose real passion was climbing; he visited Skye often and developed many routes in the Cuillin with Mackenzie, as well as improving the mapping for the range. He spent his last years living in the Sligachan Hotel. Both men have a Cuillin summit named in their honour.

A path is followed along Glen Sligachan, soon leaving the crowds behind; this dramatic glen is the domain of red deer and golden eagles. The path is clear but can be boggy at times, with the flanks of the Red Cuillin on one side and the Black Cuillin on the other. The objective, Marsco, is in sight throughout; a burn is followed uphill to reach a bealach from which the easiest route up to the main ridge is found.

The climb is steep, and it becomes more indistinct as height is gained. A last pull up a very steep, grassy slope leads to the main ridge of Marsco. The final stretch is a delight – the broad ridge gradually narrowing to a sharp grassy arête giving a real sense of drama, but without obstacles. The summit itself is a great place from which to survey the Cuillin peaks before a return for well-deserved refreshments at the Sligachan Hotel.

MARSCO

DISTANCE: 14KM/8.7 MILES » **TOTAL ASCENT**: 772M/2,533FT » **START GR**: NG 488299 » **TIME**: ALLOW 6 HOURS
MAP: OS EXPLORER 411, SKYE: CUILLIN HILLS, 1:25,000 » **REFRESHMENTS**: SLIGACHAN HOTEL
NAVIGATION: TRICKY IN POOR CONDITIONS; STEEP AND ROCKY IN PLACES.

Directions - Marsco

S There is a small car park on the southern side of the A87 at Sligachan, just east of the river. There is further parking to the west of the river, near the hotel and bus stop; cross the old bridge from here to reach the start. To begin, **go through the gate** and up to the statue of Norman Collie and John Mackenzie, mountaineers and firm friends who undertook many of the first routes in the Cuillin in the late nineteenth century. **Continue past the statue** and **take the path on the left** to head up Glen Sligachan.

2 **Stay on the path** as it follows a fence alongside the Allt Daraich gorge. **Ignore a gate on the left**, instead continue ahead over a pitched section of path. Continue up the glen; the path becomes wetter and rougher as the surroundings become more remote. Marsco is seen straight ahead, with the craggy silhouette of Sgùrr nan Gillean to the right and the Red Cuillin to the left. Cross several small streams until the broader Allt na Measarroch is reached.

3 **Turn left** here instead of crossing the ford and follow the smaller path upstream. This section is eroded and can be very boggy. After approximately 1km **start to climb** more steeply, with the path now close to the remains of an old fence and still alongside the water. The crag on the nose of Marsco looks impressive from here. **Keep following the burn** to reach its source on the Màm a' Phobuill, the shoulder between Marsco and Beinn Dearg Mheadhonach. It is said that Bonnie Prince Charlie crossed this pass at night during his epic walk from Portree to Elgol, fleeing pursuing troops.

4 **Turn right** here and stay on the path which continues to **follow the old fence posts**. Cross the lower ground to the base of Coire nan Laogh. The corrie sits between two steep ridges sweeping down from the summit ridge. **Cross the stream and continue following the fence posts**, climbing more steeply up the ridge on the eastern side of the corrie. The path peters out in places; **keep climbing** and enjoy the fabulous views of Blàbheinn and nearby Garbh-bheinn. **Bear slightly left** near the top to leave the ridge, which becomes increasingly difficult and scree-covered. Instead, climb up close to the line of iron fence posts on very steep grass, which can be slippery when wet.

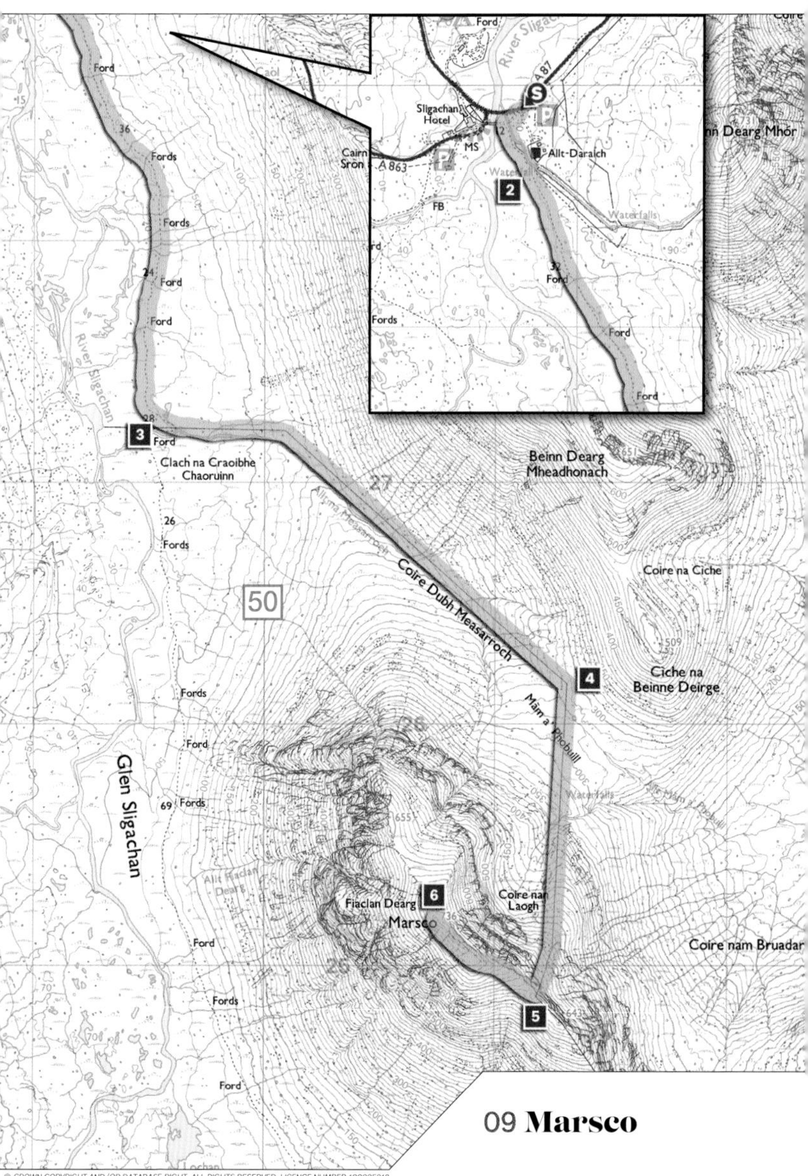
Ford
Fords
Fords
Ford
Ford
Sligachan Hotel
A87
S
P
Cairn Sron
A863
MS
Allt-Daraich
Waterfalls
2
FB
Waterfalls
Fords
Ford
Ford
River Sligachan
3
Ford
Clach na Craoibhe Chaoruinn
Fords
Fords
Ford
Fords
Glen Sligachan
Ford
Fords
Ford
Beinn Dearg Mheadhonach
Coire na Ciche
Coire Dubh Measarroch
4
Ciche na Beinne Deirge
Màm a' Phobuill
Waterfalls
Fiaclan Dearg
6
Marsco
Coire nan Laogh
Coire nam Bruadar
5
50

09 Marsco

Directions – Marsco continued ...

5 Emerge on to the main ridge of Marsco at its lowest point and you will immediately be rewarded with stunning views of the main Cuillin Ridge and south towards the sea. A short detour left along the ridge leads to an optional dramatic viewpoint, otherwise **turn right** to head up the broad ridge. This is the most enjoyable part of the walk, and the main climbing is also behind you. **Stay on the highest ground** as the ridge levels and narrows to a dramatic, grassy knife-edge. There isn't any scrambling or other obstacles and eventually the 736m summit is reached, with a cairn just beyond.

6 While it looks tempting to continue ahead, this north-west ridge leads to difficult crags. Instead, turn around and **head back along the summit ridge** to the rim of Coire nan Laogh. From here, **descend using the outward path**, following the line of fence posts and **turn left** to head downstream alongside the Allt na Measarroch. Once back in Glen Sligachan, **turn right** to follow the main glen path back to the start and perhaps a celebratory dram at the Sligachan Hotel, so beloved by Norman Collie.

CLOUD-CAPPED MARSCO

BLÀBHEINN FROM MARSCO

FIRST VIEW OF LOCH CORUISK

10 Sgùrr na Strì

23.3km/14.5 miles

The remote 494-metre summit of Sgùrr na Strì offers what many regard as the finest summit view in all Scotland.

Sligachan » Allt na Measarroch » Lochan Dubha » watershed path junction » Druim Hain cairn » Sgùrr na Strì » Druim Hain cairn » watershed path junction » Lochan Dubha » Allt na Measarroch » Sligachan

Start

Sligachan Old Bridge car park, A87 (just east of the bridge over the River Sligachan). Additional parking available west of the bridge. GR: NG 488299.

The Walk

This low outlier of the Cuillin has become renowned by photographers and landscape lovers in recent years for its unmatched view of the great ridge across the gulf of Loch Coruisk. Although still a rugged outing with pathless, rocky terrain high up, the approach we describe here from Sligachan is more straightforward than the alternative, shorter route from Kilmarie, and has only minimal scrambling.

The path up Glen Sligachan leads into remote terrain, passing between the Black Cuillin and the Red Cuillin. The going is fairly level, soon giving views into Harta Corrie, said to be the site of a legendary battle in the long-running feud between the MacDonald and MacLeod clans. It is said that when the MacDonalds attacked, the battle raged here all day; when all the MacLeods had been slaughtered, their bodies were stacked up against a boulder known as the Bloody Stone.

Today all is peaceful, and continuing up the glen, the route offers superb views of the hidden side of Blàbheinn, eventually reaching a path junction marked by a large cairn. From here the walk gets much more strenuous, with a climb up to the pass overlooking Loch Coruisk, and then a yomp over increasingly rough and pathless ground to reach the summit of Sgùrr na Strì.

There are seemingly endless sea views out to the Small Isles and Mull, but it is the close-up views of the Cuillin peaks rising from in a fantastical arc behind glistening Loch Coruisk that is the real showstopper. This really is a walk to keep for a fine day. The return is by the same outward descent and back along Glen Sligachan.

SGÙRR NA STRÌ

DISTANCE: 23.3KM/14.5 MILES » **TOTAL ASCENT**: 726M/2,382FT » **START GR**: NG 488299 » **TIME**: ALLOW 8 HOURS
MAP: OS EXPLORER 411, SKYE: CUILLIN HILLS, 1:25,000 » **REFRESHMENTS**: SLIGACHAN HOTEL
NAVIGATION: FINAL ASCENT ON ROUGH GROUND NEEDS GOOD MAP READING SKILLS.

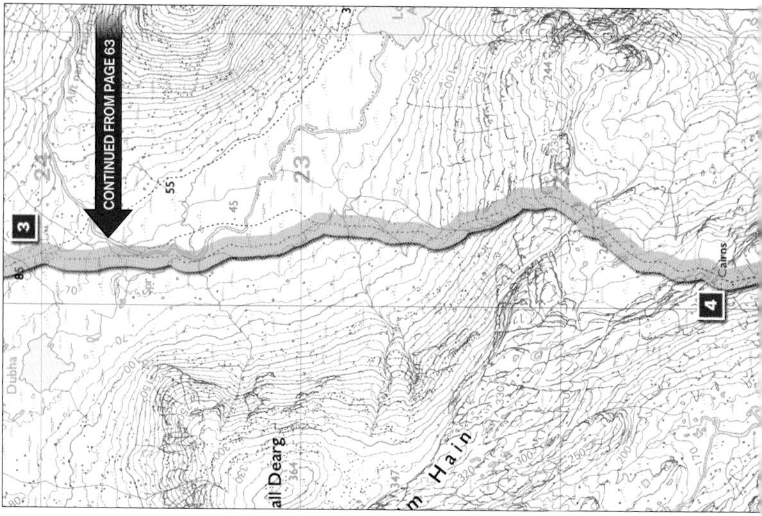
CONTINUED FROM PAGE 63
3
4
Cairns
Dubha
all Dearg
364
347
m Hain

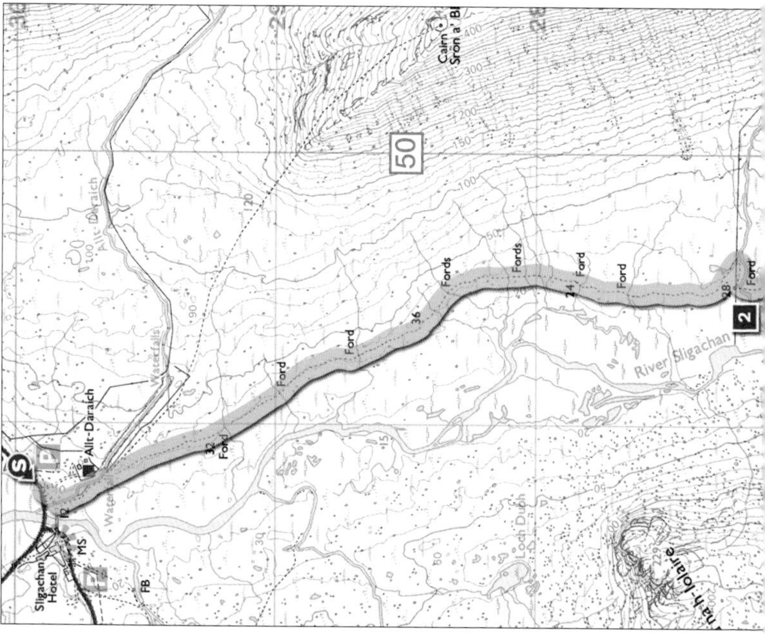
S
P
Sligachan Hotel
MS
FB
Allt-Daraich
Waterfalls
Ford
Fords
Cairn
Sròn a' Bh
50
River Sligachan
Loch Dubh
2
na h-Iolaire

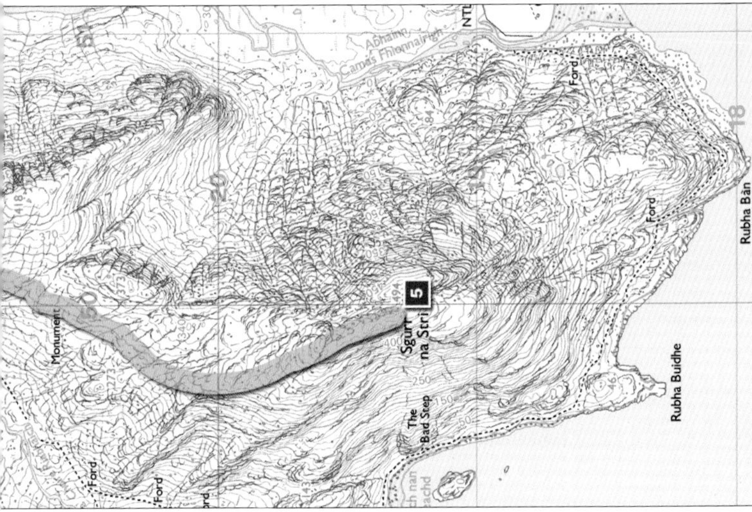

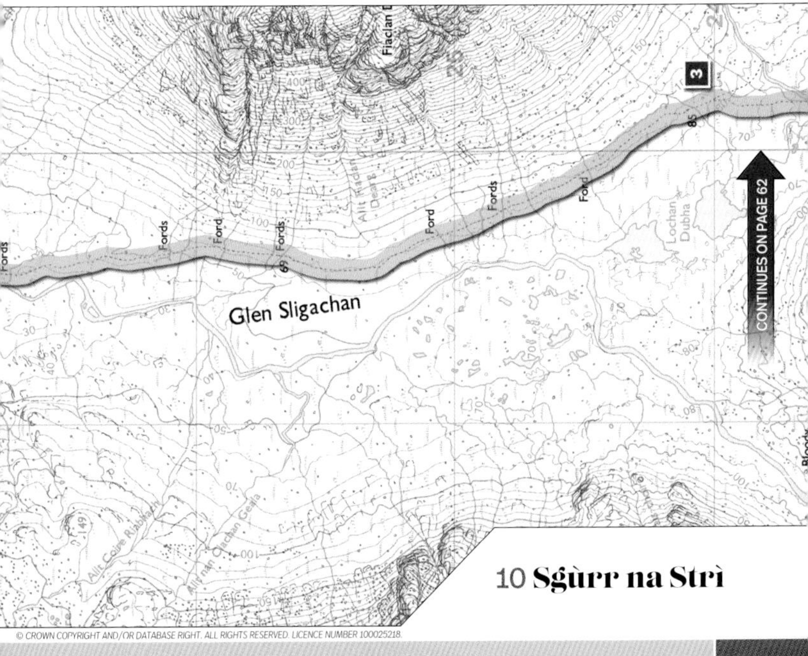

10 Sgùrr na Strì

CONTINUES ON PAGE 62

Directions – Sgùrr na Strì

S→ There is a small car park on the southern side of the A87 at Sligachan, just east of the river. There is further parking to the west of the river, near the hotel and bus stop; cross the old bridge from here to reach the start. To begin, **go through the gate** and up to the statue of mountaineering pioneers Norman Collie and John Mackenzie. **Continue past the statue** and **take the path on the left** to head up Glen Sligachan, soon following a fence. Ignore a gate on the left and **continue on the path**, which leads up Glen Sligachan. **Cross a number of small streams** and, as the hustle and bustle of Sligachan falls away, the path becomes more remote with good views to Sgùrr nan Gillean to the right and the Red Cuillin and Marsco to the left.

2 **After 3km cross the Allt na Measarroch** on big stepping stones. **Stay on the path** heading along the glen, crossing a boggy area before it improves underfoot. After around 3km, Lochan Dubha is passed on the right and the Cuillin mountains of Sgùrr Dubh Mòr, Sgùrr Alasdair and Sgùrr Dearg come into view. The fin of rock protruding from Sgùrr Dearg is known as the In Pinn or the Inaccessible Pinnacle, and is regarded as the hardest Munro, requiring ropes and a mastery of fear of heights to get to the top. (The walk to the bottom of the In Pinn is described in walk 14.)

3 Continue on the path over a slight watershed and soon afterwards **fork right** at a large cairn with views to Blàbheinn ahead to the left. **Cross a stream** and soon **start climbing** as the path heads up the right-hand side of the glen aiming for a col with a tiny lochan; Sgùrr Hain is the conical peak ahead, hiding Sgùrr na Strì.

4 Continue climbing to reach the Druim Hain ridge at a large cairn, with a first view of Loch Coruisk below. **Branch left** off the main path here (the main path leads down to Loch Coruisk). Over to the right and behind you, the slender summit and pinnacles of Sgùrr nan Gillean look spectacular. **Follow a rough path** which traverses the slopes below Sgùrr Hain before descending slightly over rough ground to reach the foot of Sgùrr na Strì; by this point the path has disappeared completely. **Keep to the right of a stream** and **climb south up a broad ridge,** crossing a number of rock slabs before reaching the summit cairn.

5 Marking the 494m western summit of Sgùrr na Strì, the cairn has a truly memorable summit view. Out to sea, the islands of Eigg, Rùm and Mull can be made out and the jagged peaks of the Cuillin Ridge curving round Loch Coruisk are magical on a good day. From near the cliff edge there are almost aerial views of the loch with two lovely sandy bays shining out below. If you want to reach the highest point, you will need to scramble down and up to the eastern summit, 200m away, which has a good views down to Camasunary. After enjoying the views, the return is by the same long outward route. **Head back down** to the Druim Hain cairn, **keep right** here to descend into Glen Sligachan and **head north along the glen path** to return to Sligachan aiming for the white dot which eventually comes into view as the Sligachan Hotel.

VIEW FROM THE SUMMIT OF SGÙRR NA STRÌ

GLAMAIG FROM SLIGACHAN

11 Glamaig & the Red Cuillin

12.5km/7.8 miles

This tough horseshoe hillwalk, with fabulous sea and mountain views, finishes on the punishing screes of Glamaig, famous for its hill race.

Sligachan » Druim na Ruaige » Beinn Dearg Mheadhonach » Bealach Mosgaraidh » Beinn Dearg Mhór » Bealach na Sgàirde » Glamaig » Bealach na Sgàirde » Allt Daraich » Sligachan

Start

Sligachan Old Bridge car park, A87 (just east of the bridge over the River Sligachan). Additional parking available west of the bridge. GR: NG 488299.

The Walk

The route starts from Sligachan, where the view of the Cuillin is one of the most photographed in Scotland. Glamaig attracts less attention, but looks every bit as steep and arduous as it turns out to be; it is the objective of an annual hill race which sees a curious mix of elite mountain runners, intrepid locals and chancers tackle the slopes head-on. They are enthusiastically cheered by supporters at the Sligachan Hotel. The race commemorates a Sherpa, Harkabir Thapa, who ran up and down from the hotel bar in 1899 in 55 minutes. Today's top finishers are only slightly faster, and none of them do it barefoot, as Thapa is said to have done.

The walk begins by passing the sculpture of Norman Collie and John Mackenzie, and then follows a pretty gorge and tumbling stream for a short distance before striking off across moorland on a very boggy path. Climbing up a broad ridge, there are increasingly good views across Glen Sligachan to the Cuillin. The route up to the first peak, Beinn Dearg Mheadhonach, is a relatively easy introduction, with only a short section of scree before the cairn and summit are reached. Enjoy a quick stop to take in the mountain and sea views before a straightforward descent and climb to the next summit, Beinn Dearg Mhór.

From here the walk takes on a much rockier and more challenging nature. The descent starts easily enough, but then becomes steep and loose, before the final, long climb to the summit of Glamaig. The amazing views from the top can help you forget your aching limbs. Although you can choose to descend directly using the shorter race route, the walk takes a slightly easier route returning via the col and then descending over moorland and bog to rejoin the outward path.

GLAMAIG & THE RED CUILLIN

DISTANCE: 12.5KM/7.8 MILES » **TOTAL ASCENT**: 1,182M/3,878FT » **START GR**: NG 488299 » **TIME**: ALLOW 8 HOURS
MAP: OS EXPLORER 411, SKYE: CUILLIN HILLS, 1:25,000 » **REFRESHMENTS**: SLIGACHAN HOTEL
NAVIGATION: PATHLESS IN PLACES; GOOD NAVIGATION SKILLS NEEDED IN POOR VISIBILITY; STEEP SCREE.

Directions – Glamaig & the Red Cuillin

S There is a small car park on the southern side of the A87 at Sligachan, just east of the river. There is further parking to the west of the river, near the hotel and bus stop; cross the old bridge from here to reach the start. To begin, **go through the gate** and up to the statue of early mountaineers Norman Collie and John Mackenzie. **Continue past the statue** and **take the path on the left**. After 300m **turn left through a gate** and follow the path alongside the Allt Daraich gorge. **Stay on the main path** and ignore a path on the right. Soon **turn left** on to a smaller path leading to a gate.

2 **Continue ahead** across rougher ground and **follow the line of metal fence posts**; the path is boggy. The path becomes fainter; **aim south-east** directly towards the Druim na Ruaige ridge of Beinn Dearg Mheadhonach, where a path can be seen climbing ahead. The flattish ground before the ridge can be extremely boggy underfoot. **Climb the path**, which is steep at first until the flatter shoulder of the Druim na Ruaige is reached. Follow the path which zigzags up the steep stony slope ahead to eventually **reach the cairn** on Beinn Dearg Mheadhonach. Translating from Gaelic as the 'middle red mountain', the actual summit is a 300m detour to the right along the ridge.

3 Return to the first cairn then **aim north to follow a broad ridge downhill**; there is a path. From the low point, the Bealach Mosgaraidh, **climb steeply** ahead to the summit of Beinn Dearg Mhór. At 731m, this is rightly named the 'big red mountain' and is another excellent viewpoint both to the Cuillin and over the sea to the Isle of Raasay and the mountains of the west coast of the Scottish mainland.

4 **Keep heading north (downhill)** from the summit; the going is gentle for 500m until a cairn marks the abrupt steepening of the surrounding slopes. From the cairn, **turn sharp left** and go back on yourself for a few steps before **bearing right on a faint path** which plunges down the stony hillside. **Zigzag down the scree path**, aiming directly for the Bealach na Sgàirde* – this is the steepest section of the walk.

SC * The walk can be shortened by descending to the left from the Bealach na Sgàirde, avoiding the ascent of Glamaig and following the directions from towards the end of **6**.

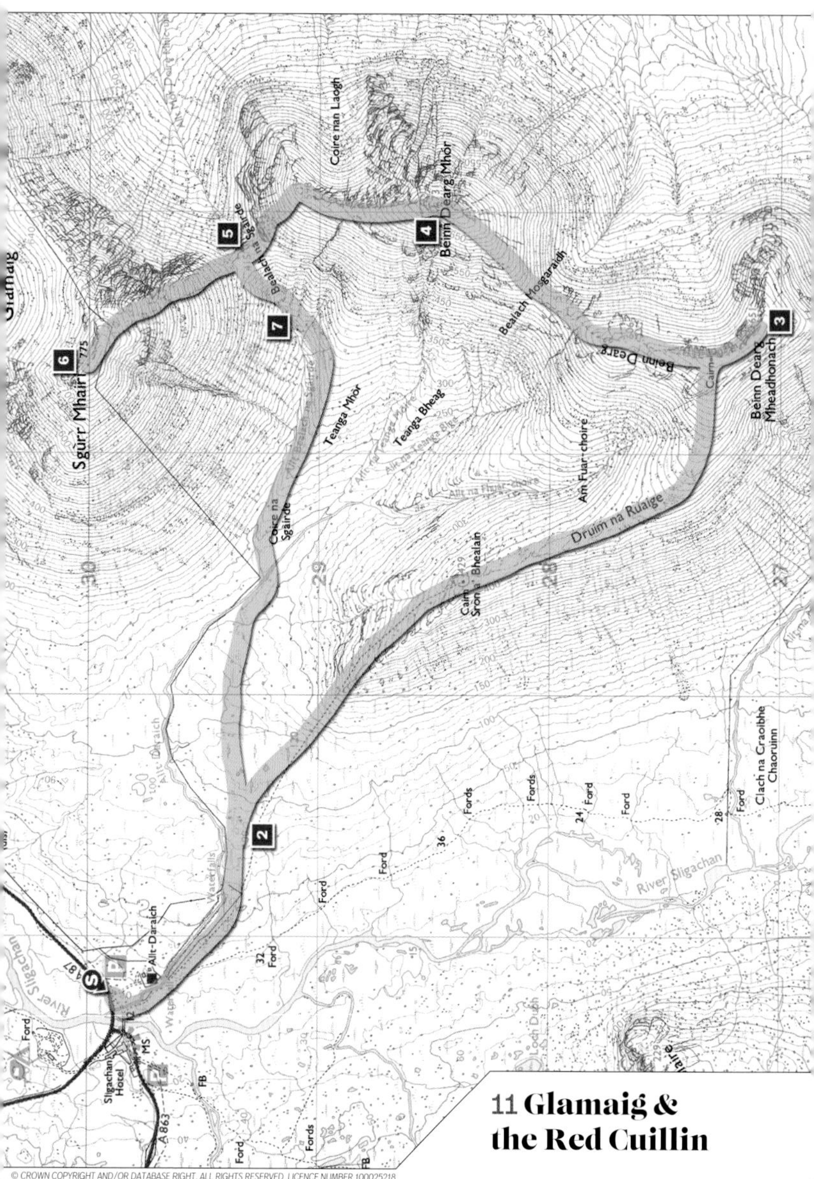

11 Glamaig & the Red Cuillin

Directions – Glamaig & the Red Cuillin continued ...

5 If heading up Glamaig, **pick up the faint path on the left-hand side** of the intimidating slope directly ahead. **Climb very steeply** on a mix of scree and grass, with zigzags making the ascent slightly easier. Eventually the 775m summit of mighty Glamaig is reached, marked by a cairn. The views from this conical mountain do not disappoint – the dramatic Black Cuillin to the west and a panorama of islands and coast in all other directions.

6 It is possible to descend directly towards Sligachan from the summit, but it is extremely punishing, on very slippery scree, with no real path and then across rough, boggy ground. It is easier to turn around and **retrace the route back down** to the Bealach na Sgàirde. From the low point **turn right** and descend the steep heather between more eroded sections of the slope. There are hints of a path in places. Nearer the bottom **aim diagonally left** to cross the stream and **join the lower of the two paths** visible, crossing the low slope ahead.

7 Cross the heathery slope on the path which gently rises to reach the Teanga Mhòr ridge; **turn right** here. **Continue down this ridge** on the path and **cross the Allt Daraich** just before the Allt Bealach na Sgàirde joins it. On the far side, **turn right** following a boggy path for 100m before **aiming diagonally left to bear directly west** across wet, rough and pathless ground to eventually join the outward route. Once back at the path coming down from Beinn Dearg Mheadhonach, **turn right**. From here, retrace your steps back to the start. **Go through the gate** and at the path junction **turn right**. **Keep on the main path** to return through the metal gate and back to the statue and Sligachan.

VIEW FROM BEINN DEARG MHÓR

WATERFALL ON THE ALLT DARAICH

AM BÀSTEIR FROM THE BEALACH NAN LICE

12 Bruach na Frìthe

14km/8.7 miles

This fine peak would be more celebrated in any other surroundings; the perfect introduction to the Cuillin Ridge.

Sligachan » Allt Dearg Mòr » Fionn Choire » Bealach nan Lice » Sgùrr a' Bhàsteir » Bealach nan Lice » Sgùrr a' Fhionn Choire » Bruach na Frìthe » Allt Dearg Mòr » Sligachan

Start

Lay-by on the A863, 700m west of Sligachan. GR: NG 480297.

The Walk

Perhaps the best introduction to the drama and challenge of the Cuillin, Bruach na Frìthe is one of the finest viewpoints on the whole ridge. Although only very minor scrambling is needed, this route can still be very intimidating for those not yet used to the bare rock walls and scale of the Cuillin; route finding can be tricky especially in bad weather. We describe an optional return route down the north-west ridge, or you can retrace your steps for an easier option. If you are looking for more of a challenge, you could reverse the route and take in more optional scrambling by ascending this ridge.

The walk begins along a track just over half a kilometre from the road junction at Sligachan, but soon turns on to a path, running above a delightful burn with many waterfalls and beautiful pools. It climbs gently towards the pass to Glen Brittle, but near the top the route swings left to head towards and into Fionn Choire. From the upper reaches of a corrie, a steep scree path leads up to the main Cuillin Ridge at a spectacular location overlooked by the Bàsteir Tooth.

A detour out along a narrow ridge to Sgùrr a' Bhàsteir gives even better views, with the pinnacle ridge of Sgùrr nan Gillean revealed in its full majesty. Back on the main route, Bruach na Frìthe itself is reached by a scrambly route below and then along the main ridge of the Cuillin, a steep final pull bringing you to the trig point at the summit. The optional descent via the north-west ridge has trickier route finding, but most of the scrambling on the crest can be bypassed via scree paths on the left. If unsure, you can instead retrace your steps for the return. A pint at the cavernous walkers' bar at the Sligachan Hotel is usually considered part of the achievement.

BRUACH NA FRÌTHE

DISTANCE: 14KM/8.7 MILES » **TOTAL ASCENT**: 944M/3,097FT » **START GR**: NG 480297 » **TIME**: ALLOW 7 HOURS
MAP: OS EXPLORER 411, SKYE: CUILLIN HILLS, 1:25,000 » **REFRESHMENTS**: SLIGACHAN HOTEL
NAVIGATION: VERY TRICKY IN POOR WEATHER; GOOD NAVIGATION SKILLS AND EXPERIENCE NEEDED; SOME EASY SCRAMBLING.

Directions – Bruach na Frìthe

S From the junction at the Sligachan Hotel, take the road towards Dunvegan to a marked parking lay-by on the left, just beyond where a track leaves the A863. **Follow the track heading towards a white cottage** (Alltdearg House); **turn right** on to a footpath just before the cottage. Follow the path by the Allt Dearg Mòr, heading gently uphill and passing a number of waterfalls and clear pools. As height is gained, Sgùrr nan Gillean's pinnacle ridge comes into view, looking much finer than from Sligachan.

2 Approximately 3km from the start **turn left** at a fork in the path. The path is now fainter and boggier. Soon **keep left** again at a second fork and **ford a small burn**, now aiming directly towards Fionn Choire. **Cross the rock-strewn grass of the lower slopes of Fionn Choire**, with the summit of Bruach na Frìthe now visible ahead on the right. **Keep going straight ahead uphill**, aiming towards the shoulder on the mountain ridge. The path becomes much fainter as the rocky higher bowl of the upper corrie is reached. Pick up the clearer path and **climb the scree on the left-hand side** of the corrie.

LOOKING BACK FROM THE ASCENT TO THE SUMMIT

12 Bruach na Frìthe

Directions - Bruach na Frìthe continued ...

3 **Climb steeply** to reach the Bealach nan Lice, a dramatic point on the Cuillin Ridge sandwiched between the improbable Bàsteir Tooth and the rocky boss of Sgùrr a' Fhionn Choire. On a clear day it's worth making an out-and-back detour along a short spur ridge to Sgùrr a' Bhàsteir. To do this, **head up to the left and then aim left** away from the Bàsteir Tooth along the ridge. **Keep on the ridge, heading north**; there is some easy down-scrambling early on and then the route follows the narrower ridge and climbs up to the dramatic viewpoint at the summit.

4 Retrace your route back to Bealach nan Lice. From the bealach, **follow a scree path to the right** (south-west) of Sgùrr a' Fhionn Choire at first and **keep just to the right of the main ridge** to stay on the easiest ground for a short distance. **Return to the main ridge**, which now leads west, and climb directly up scree towards Bruach na Frìthe. **Stay to the left of low crags** on the final steep climb up to the summit.

5 At 958m, this is the only summit on the Cuillin Ridge to be marked with a trig point. The easiest descent is to **return to the start via the outward route**; however, if you are feeling confident the north-west ridge provides an alternative*.

OR * This optional route involves some moderate scrambling and careful navigation, but any difficult obstacles can be bypassed. **Bear north-west and keep just to the left of the main ridge** to head downhill on very rough, steep and loose ground. The scrambling on the ridge can be avoided by walking on the scree on the left. About a third of the way down the route squeezes between a large rock and the ridge and then follows the eroded line of basalt faults providing groove-like paths to scramble down. Once the gradient becomes less steep, **follow a narrow section of ridge**. Before the ground becomes much steeper again, **bear slightly right to head down the north ridge**, aiming for the grassy ground of Fionn Choire. From here, **pick up the outward route** to return to the Allt Dearg Mòr and follow it back to the start.

RED HILLS FROM BRUACH NA FRÌTHE

VIEW TO LOCH CORUISK FROM THE SUMMIT

13 Sgùrr na Banachdaich

7.3km/4.5 miles

Though one of the easier of Skye's Cuillin Munros to climb, this remains an exceptionally rugged route compared to hillwalking on the mainland. The summit views over Loch Coruisk are sensational.

Glenbrittle Youth Hostel » Allt a' Choire Ghreadaidh » Allt Coir' an Eich » An Diallaid » Sgùrr na Banachdaich » An Diallaid » Allt Coir' an Eich » Allt a' Choire Ghreadaidh » Glenbrittle Youth Hostel

Start

Lay-by opposite Glenbrittle Youth Hostel, Glen Brittle. GR: NG 409225.

The Walk

From Glen Brittle, the Cuillin looks extremely intimidating, but this route up to the midpoint on the ridge is one of the few ascents without significant scrambling; it's extremely rough and rocky, and requires careful navigation, but still remains a fine introduction to these alpine-like peaks.

There is a rough parking area opposite the youth hostel part way down Glen Brittle. From here the walk climbs gently at first by a rushing burn, passing a number of waterfalls, much quieter than the nearby Fairy Pools. Soon the route leaves the main path to strike out across boggy moorland, climbing up towards the scree-filled corrie below Sgùrr na Banachdaich. The Gaelic name means 'smallpox peak', and it's thought that it may refer to the pockmarked appearance given by the endless stones.

The route becomes much steeper as it heads up towards the crag of An Diallaid. From here the going is extremely rocky but there are no major difficulties; any obstacles can be easily avoided. A short distance leads to a col below Sgùrr na Banachdaich, and a dramatic viewpoint out to the sharp peaks of Sgùrr a' Ghreadaidh. The final climb is steep, up a broad, rocky ridge, leading to the airy summit with fabulous views along the main Cuillin Ridge towards the Inaccessible Pinnacle and Sgùrr Alasdair as well as down to the jewel-like waters of Loch Coruisk far below. The return is by the same outward route, with grand views over Glen Brittle and its bay.

SGÙRR NA BANACHDAICH

DISTANCE: 7.3KM/4.5 MILES » **TOTAL ASCENT**: 912M/2,992FT » **START GR**: NG 409225 » **TIME**: ALLOW 6 HOURS **MAP**: OS EXPLORER 411, SKYE: CUILLIN HILLS, 1:25,000 » **REFRESHMENTS**: GLENBRITTLE CAMPSITE CAFE; TAIGH AILEAN HOTEL, PORTNALONG » **NAVIGATION**: CAREFUL ROUTE FINDING NEEDED, ESPECIALLY IN POOR VISIBILITY.

Directions – Sgùrr na Banachdaich

S From the lay-by opposite the youth hostel **take the path towards the Cuillin**, following the south bank of the Allt a' Choire Ghreadaidh; the path is good underfoot. Soon the route passes a couple of impressive waterfalls, and the path keeps above the rim of a gorge. There are a few accessible pools which would provide a refreshing dip on descent on a hot summer's day.

2 **After just over 1km turn right** on to a much fainter and boggier path; a tiny cairn marks the junction, but it is easily missed as the main path carries on alongside the stream. **Continue ahead** as the path becomes clearer to follow. **Head uphill**, passing a large boulder and crossing the open moorland. After wet weather it can be very boggy underfoot. **Climb to the top of a rise** and continue on the path as the gradient eases. From here the route ahead is clearly seen. The pointy peak to the left of the scree-filled Coir' an Eich is An Diallaid, a prominent crag on a ridge which leads to the summit of Sgùrr na Banachdaich. The right-hand side of the corrie is dominated by Sgùrr nan Gobhar, itself linked to Sgùrr na Banachdaich by an airy arête. **Follow the path**, now very indistinct, and **bear slightly left** towards the stream flowing from Coir' an Eich.

3 **Cross the Allt Coir' an Eich** and **head directly up the pathless, grassy slopes** leading up towards An Diallaid. The ground becomes increasingly stony and there are eventually small sections of path. While it is possible to stay lower and then climb up the back of the Coir' an Eich, the latter route is plagued by scree, and the climb via An Diallaid is more enjoyable. **Keep climbing** as the slope eases and becomes grassier for a while before steepening for the final, very steep climb to the An Diallaid crag. **Follow traces of a path** through the stones to reach this fine viewpoint, or you can bypass it to the right.

4 From the top of An Diallaid, **aim south-east** along the main ridge leading towards Sgùrr na Banachdaich, picking a way through the rocks while keeping the rim of the cliffs that fall to Coire a' Ghreadaidh close by on your left. **Cross the col** between the two peaks and **start the final climb** up to Sgùrr na Banachdaich. After the col, the easiest ground lies slightly to the right of the ridge, but careful navigation is needed up this broad, rocky slope which has little sense of exposure. **Keep heading directly for the 965m summit**.

5 This is the halfway point of the celebrated Cuillin Ridge, and on a good day the views are sensational. Though the summit feels more airy than the ground crossed to get here, there are plenty of spots to sit and enjoy the vista, taking in the yawning void of Loch Coruisk to the east, or along the ridge to Sgùrr Dearg and the Inaccessible Pinnacle to the south, or the sharp peaks of Sgùrr Thormaid and the Three Teeth to Sgùrr a' Ghreadaidh to the north. **Retrace your steps to return**, enjoying fantastic views down Glen Brittle to the sea the whole way; all other possible routes involve much more scrambling or steep, loose scree.

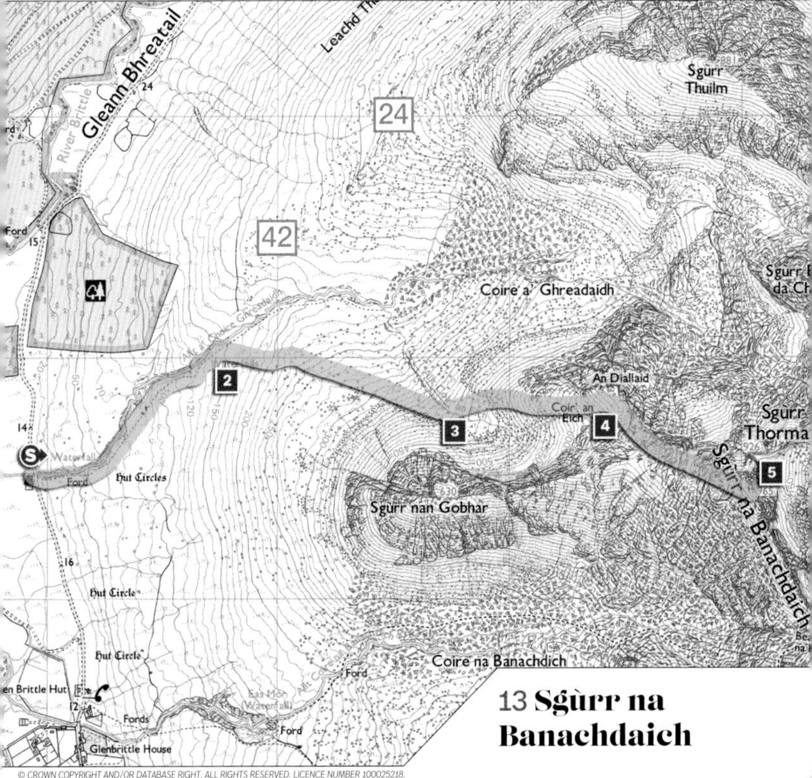

13 Sgùrr na Banachdaich

THE IN PINN SEEN FROM SGÙRR DEARG SUMMIT

14 Sgùrr Dearg & the Inaccessible Pinnacle

7.5km/4.7 miles

This extremely rugged route reaches the base of the famous Inaccessible Pinnacle, one of the most dramatic locations in Scotland's mountains.

Glen Brittle Memorial Hut » Allt Coire na Banachdich » Eas Mòr » Coire na Banachdich » Bealach Coire na Banachdich » Inaccessible Pinnacle » Sgùrr Dearg western ridge » Eas Mòr » Allt Coire na Banachdich » Glen Brittle Memorial Hut

Start

Small car park opposite the Glen Brittle Memorial Hut, Glen Brittle. GR: NG 411216.

The Walk

Despite its short distance, this is an extremely rough and challenging walk, involving very careful route finding and some straightforward scrambling. The reward is a visit to a truly awe-inspiring location – the base of the Inaccessible Pinnacle, the only Munro that requires rock climbing to reach its highest point.

Beginning with a sea-level start in Glen Brittle, a good path crosses grazing land and climbs alongside a deep gorge. The character of the walk changes as the terrain underfoot becomes rockier on the path up into Coire na Banachdich. Fearsome cliffs eventually rear up ahead; there's no direct route to the pass at the back of the corrie and the route to get there requires some very complex and careful route finding. Once above the first tiers of cliffs, the route traverses scree before climbing again to reach the Bealach Coire na Banachdich, the lowest point on the entire Cuillin Ridge. A very short, easy initial scramble gives access to a broad but rocky ridge ascending to reach Sgùrr Dearg. The summit is overtopped by the incredible Inaccessible Pinnacle. From here you can watch rock climbers ascending the narrow fin of rock and abseiling down the steeper side almost to your feet. An ascent of the pinnacle itself must be left to those with mountaineering skills and equipment.

The descent from Sgùrr Dearg requires more scrambling and again some tricky route finding at first before it follows, and sometimes traverses, the flanks of a rocky ridge. There are great views over the Rubha an Dùnain peninsula and distant islands. Eventually the grey rock gives way to the green of Glen Brittle and the outward path is rejoined for the final amble.

SGÙRR DEARG & THE INACCESSIBLE PINNACLE

DISTANCE: 7.5KM/4.7 MILES » **TOTAL ASCENT**: 939M/3,081FT » **START GR**: NG 411216 » **TIME**: ALLOW 8 HOURS **MAP**: OS EXPLORER 411, SKYE: CUILLIN HILLS, 1:25,000 » **REFRESHMENTS**: GLENBRITTLE CAMPSITE CAFE; TAIGH AILEAN HOTEL, PORTNALONG » **NAVIGATION**: DIFFICULT ROUTE FINDING WITH SOME SCRAMBLING; GOOD NAVIGATION SKILLS NEEDED.

Directions – Sgùrr Dearg & the Inaccessible Pinnacle

S Heading down Glen Brittle towards the sea, there is a small car park opposite the Glen Brittle Memorial Hut, itself just beyond the Mountain Rescue Post. **Walk down the road for 50m and turn left** before some livestock pens. Follow the path up and **cross the bridge** over the Allt Coire na Banachdich and **continue uphill** on the far side. Soon the path reveals a spectacular view of the 40-metre-high Eas Mòr waterfall pouring down the tree-lined gorge.

2 After the gorge **turn left when the path forks**, heading slightly downhill before continuing up into the large corrie. **Keep climbing on the path**, which becomes much rougher as the ground changes from grass to rock. **Stay on the right-hand side of the corrie**, eventually heading up a wide gully leading to the upper part of Coire na Banachdich.

3 After **crossing a small burn, bear right** to climb up the far bank on a faint path. As it steepens, **zigzag up the left-hand side between and over the rocky slabs and scree**. There are a few cairns, but care is needed to find the best line. Keep climbing and eventually **bear right** to reach a wide, stony gully which leads up to the right (south) of the corrie headwall. **Climb up this gully**; there are small cairns as it narrows. **Bear right near the top on a faint path** on a terrace. Keep climbing up the more broken ground ahead and then, where the route towards the ridge is blocked by cliffs, **traverse left, keeping below the cliffs**. Ignore the scree gullies above that look like they might provide quick access to the ridge – they don't – and keep traversing across the boulders and scree; there is a faint path in places. **Descend slightly** to pass below a crag at the bottom of the cliffs and continue crossing boulders and stones. Soon **bear right to climb up** to the lowest point in the ridge, Bealach Coire na Banachdich – identified by the orange sand on the ground.

4 **Scramble up the rocks to the right** to get out of the bealach and keep heading uphill as the now broader ridge climbs. **Zigzag up a faint path** on the north face of Sgùrr Dearg to reach the summit, with an amazing view of the Inaccessible Pinnacle ahead.

5 The descent route uses the west ridge of Sgùrr Dearg, with careful route finding and a little scrambling at first. **Follow the path on the right-hand side of the ridge** and soon return to the true crest. **Stay high and cross to the left-hand side** and **descend an easy gully** before **bearing right** to traverse on a clear path across the left-hand side of the ridge. In a short while, descend broken rocks to resume a path and then negotiate a short, easy gully; keep heading along this side of the ridge as the path rejoins the ridge below the top of a minor peak. **Keep on the left-hand side** but near the ridge, with sections of path, scree and rock slabs, but no real scrambling. **Stay on the path,** zigzagging down to reach the flatter ground above Window Buttress.

6 **Stay on the ridge** to reach Sròn Dearg above Loch an Fhir-bhallaich. **Continue down the ridge, taking the right-hand side at a steep section** to eventually gain a path on slightly easier ground. **Keep descending** and eventually the path rejoins the outward route. Pass the gorge and waterfall to return to the start.

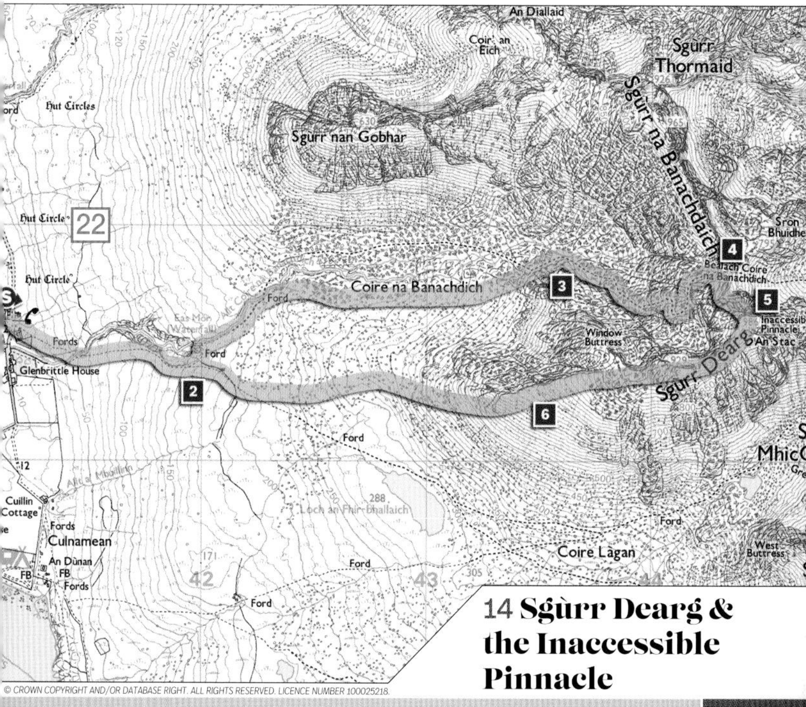

14 Sgùrr Dearg & the Inaccessible Pinnacle

Section 24

South Skye & the Isle of Raasay

The southern part of Skye – and its neighbour Raasay – offer a wonderful variety of landscapes. Here is the great outlier of the Cuillin, Blàbheinn, rising dramatically above Loch Slapin on the stunning Strathaird peninsula. Beinn na Caillich towers over Broadford, the largest settlement in the area. Further south, Sleat has some of the greenest and most fertile land on Skye.

Just a short hop on the ferry from Sconser, the neighbouring Isle of Raasay feels like a world apart from its more famous neighbour. Only a tiny proportion of Skye's many visitors venture here; the walk up to Dùn Caan, the distinctive flat-topped summit of the island, is a neglected classic.

BLÀBHEINN FROM THE ELGOL COASTAL PATH

RÙM FROM NEAR THE POINT OF SLEAT

TRACK LEADING TOWARDS THE POINT

15 Point of Sleat

8.6km/5.3 miles

The Point of Sleat, the southernmost part of Skye, is reached on this straightforward walk, which takes in a beautiful sandy beach along the way.

Aird » moorland below Sgurran Seilich » path junction » Point of Sleat » Camas Daraich » path junction » moorland below Sgurran Seilich » Aird

Start

Parking area at Aird road end.
GR: NG 588007.

The Walk

Sleat has a very different feel to much of the island – it is known as the 'garden of Skye'. At Sabhal Mòr Ostaig – part of the federal University of the Highlands and Islands – degrees and other courses are taught in Gaelic, and community-run initiatives help to keep the scattered crofting settlements viable. Once beyond Armadale, the road narrows to a long section of single-track road, eventually reaching a small parking area. From here the walk begins on a track meandering across moorland. Cattle and sheep graze here, so keep dogs under strict control.

The track crosses the rough ground with several short but steep climbs and descents before the walk turns on to a footpath. This section is rocky and boggy underfoot, but gives great views over this secluded corner of the island.

While the crofts were created in 1850, man has inhabited this spot for centuries – remains of Mesolithic life have been discovered here. After a junction the route climbs steeply again, crossing more rough ground to eventually descend to the shore at the Point of Sleat itself.

Today a modern solar-powered lighthouse has replaced the more elegant structure which was erected in 1934. The location provides vast seascapes taking in mainland Britain's most westerly peninsula, Ardnamurchan, the mountains of Knoydart, the distinctive Small Isles and Mull. Stay for a while and you may see a passing seal, whale or dolphin, or even a gannet harpooning the sea for fish.

The return is by the same route, but it is worth taking a short detour to visit the beautiful sandy bay of Camas Daraich. At low tide a wide expanse of white sand is revealed – it is a tranquil spot to rock pool, picnic or even take a bracing dip.

POINT OF SLEAT

DISTANCE: 8.6KM/5.3 MILES » **TOTAL ASCENT**: 288M/945FT » **START GR**: NG 588007 » **TIME**: ALLOW 4 HOURS
MAP: OS EXPLORER 412, SKYE: SLEAT, 1:25,000 » **REFRESHMENTS**: CAFE 1925, ARDVASAR
NAVIGATION: STRAIGHTFORWARD.

Directions – Point of Sleat

From Ardvasar take the minor road to Aird where an old church now serves as an art gallery with the parking just beyond. The track is used by local crofters; please leave space for turning and don't block any access. **Head west along the track**; pass through a wooden gate and follow the track as it climbs gently uphill. There are often livestock grazing here so keep any dogs under strict control. **Keep heading uphill** with good views to the left of the remote Knoydart Mountains across the Sound of Sleat. **Stay on the track** as it undulates across the heather moorland, traversing below the slopes of Sgurran Seilich. **Go through a gate** and continue along the track. **Descend steeply** as the track heads downhill to run alongside a stream. Ahead the mountainous island of Rùm provides a dramatic silhouette on the horizon.

2 **Cross a wooden bridge** and very soon **turn left** on to a steep, rocky path, signed *Point of Sleat*. **Climb uphill** and follow the path as it winds across the moorland staying close to a fence – it can be wet underfoot in places here. A few scattered houses come into view to the right, a mix of holiday homes and permanent residents.

3 As the path reaches a pass between two low hills, there's a junction. (The grassy path ahead leads down to the beach at Camas Daraich – a recommended detour you can save for the way back.) **Turn right** to climb uphill on a rocky path, which gives views down to the sandy bay. **Keep on the path**; eventually **go down a long flight of concrete steps** to reach the western shore. **Bear left** to reach a grassy area between two bays; the one on the left has a tiny, sandy beach. **Stay on the path** to climb up over a grass-and-bracken lump to reach the Point of Sleat and its lighthouse, which is perched on a small outcrop.

LIGHTHOUSE AT THE POINT OF SLEAT

4 This is a great place for spotting passing dolphins, seals and whales as well as cormorants and feeding gannets. The small, automated light is well positioned providing sweeping views taking in Mallaig, the Small Isles of Eigg and Rùm, the Ardnamurchan peninsula with its own much larger lighthouse and the Rubha an Dùnain peninsula below the Cuillin. **Retrace your steps to the path junction at 3 then turn right** on to a path passing a waymarker. Walk down to the sandy bay of Camas Daraich, which is a lovely spot to while away an afternoon.

5 After exploring the beach, **return to the junction at 3 and turn right**. **Retrace your steps back to the start**.

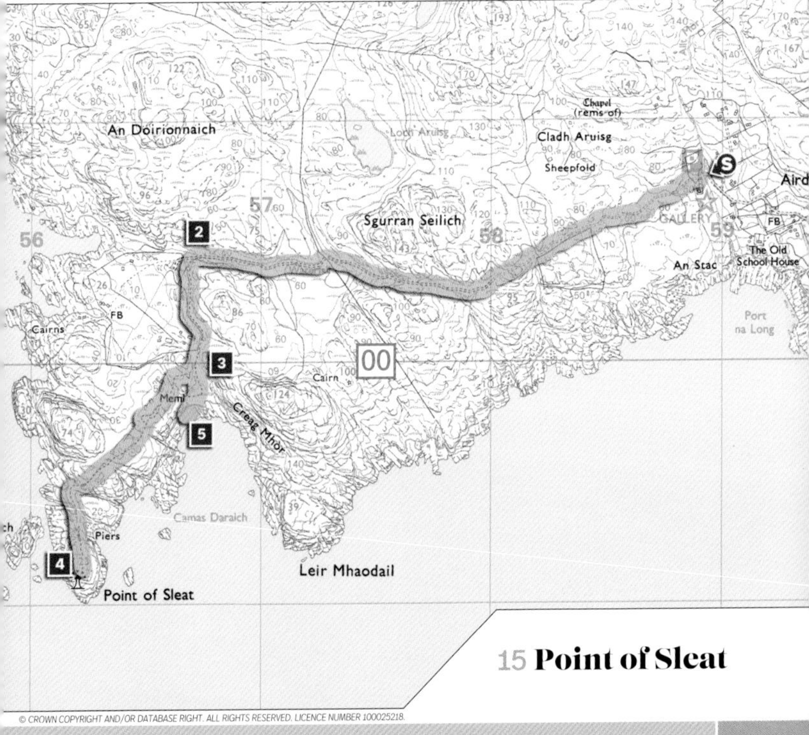

15 Point of Sleat

BROADFORD RED HILLS FROM ABOVE CILL CHRIOSD

16 Boreraig & Suisnish

16.7km/10.4 miles

Explore the heartbreaking remains of the cleared villages along the coast, and uncover Skye's marble industry.

Cill Chriosd » Beinn nan Càrn woodland » Boreraig » Suisnish » Camas Malag » B8083 » Cill Chriosd

Start

Lay-by opposite the ruins of Cill Chriosd, B8083, south-west of Broadford. GR: NG 617207.

The Walk

Starting amidst the fertile, green landscapes of Strath Suardal, the walk leaves the ruins of an old church abandoned as the population declined, and begins to climb towards a low pass. More historic signs of previous residents and industry are soon encountered as the remains of a marble quarry are passed. White Skye marble was quarried here and at other nearby sites, and in 1907 a railway line was built from a factory here to carry the processed stone to Broadford. The route then follows the line of this narrow gauge railway gently uphill before leaving it behind to follow a good path over the pass, before beginning the descent past a newly planted native woodland.

A mix of trees and open moorland leads down to the coast and the atmospheric ruins of Boreraig. At this beautiful, sheltered spot there are a number of well-preserved ruins to explore. In 1851, around 120 people lived in 22 households here, but with the textile boom in the Lowlands, the laird was keen to remove these tenants to make way for more profitable sheep. During the next year about half the population emigrated, many to Australia. The following year, Lord MacDonald forcibly cleared the remaining villagers, evicting them from their homes, many of which were burnt to the ground.

The walk continues along a scenic coast path, passing a number of impressive waterfalls, until the green fields and the remains of Suisnish are reached. Having suffered the same fate as Boreraig, only one house remained occupied by a shepherd. Now empty, this is passed on the route. The path now becomes a track and runs alongside Loch Slapin with stunning views to the Cuillin beyond. The sea is left behind at a beautiful bay, and from here the return is on the road with good views to the surrounding hills and a reed-filled loch.

BORERAIG & SUISNISH

DISTANCE: 16.7KM/10.4 MILES » **TOTAL ASCENT**: 425M/1,394FT » **START GR**: NG 617207 » **TIME**: ALLOW 6 HOURS
MAP: OS EXPLORER 412, SKYE: SLEAT, 1:25,000 » **REFRESHMENTS**: CAFE SIA OR DELI GASTA, BROADFORD; AMY'S PLACE, TORRIN » **NAVIGATION**: STRAIGHTFORWARD.

GARS-BHEINN SEEN FROM SUISNISH

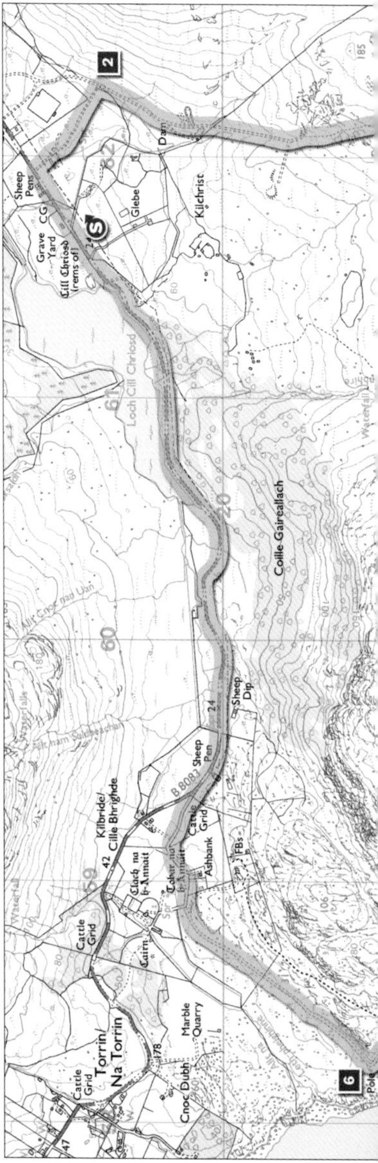

16 Boreraig & Suisnish

Directions - Boreraig & Suisnish

S There is a lay-by opposite the ruins of Cill Chriosd, about halfway between Broadford and Torrin. From here, **walk along the road** towards Broadford for 500m. **Turn right on to a track** and keep to the left of the ruins of a factory used for processing the Skye marble quarried nearby. Head gently uphill on the rough track to reach a junction.

2 **Turn right** on to a clear footpath. This is the disused railway line which once carried the marble to Broadford. While the quarries had operated for at least a century, the marble line only ran for around 5 years until the quarries closed in 1912. Continue heading uphill and **go through a gate**, passing old spoil heaps and the remains of a winding wheel used for pulling the railway carts up the slope. **Continue up to a cairn** marking the summit of the small pass; there are great views to Blàbheinn from here. The path narrows; **go through a gate** where the Beinn nan Càrn native woodland is becoming established.

3 **Stay on the path** which climbs briefly, then **descend towards the coast**. **Keep to the right of some old sheepfolds** and head towards the sea. The ruins here are the remains of the village of Boreraig, which was forcibly cleared of its residents in the mid-nineteenth century.

4 **Turn right** through the ruins and pick up the coastal path heading west. Stay on the path which passes a number of waterfalls cascading down from the cliffs to the right and has good views over the sea. Follow the path as it climbs and reaches a fence. **Turn right alongside the fence** and, after a corner, **turn left through a gate** and aim for a barn below. **Go through a gate** to the right of the barn and follow the track to a ruined house.

5 Other ruins can be seen on the surrounding hillside, these once made up the village of Suisnish, which was cleared at the same time as Boreraig; many of the residents emigrated although some of the elderly and infirm ended up in a poorhouse. **Stay on the track** for the next 3km as it follows the coast. As it heads along Loch Slapin, the Cuillin Hills provide a jagged landscape over the water. Continue to the pebbly bay of Camas Malag, an idyllic spot backed by grassy turf and with fabulous views across the water to the mountains.

6 **Take the minor road** heading uphill away from the sea. Pass the entrance to the only marble quarry still operating and continue to the road junction. **Turn right** on to the B8083. Although the road can get busy in summer it does pass the beautiful Loch Cill Chriosd, a favourite with photographers. If time allows it's well worth wandering around the graveyard at Cill Chroisd itself.

RUINS OF BORERAIG

DÙN CAAN

17 Dùn Caan, Isle of Raasay

15.5km/9.6 miles

The distinctive, flat summit of this volcanic peak dominates the small Isle of Raasay and offers sensational views.

Raasay ferry terminal » Inverarish » Inverarish Burn » Loch na Mna » Loch na Meilich » Dùn Caan » Loch na Meilich » minor road » Raasay House » Raasay ferry terminal

Start

Raasay ferry terminal, Churchton Bay, Isle of Raasay (25-minute crossing from Sconser on Skye). GR: NG 545362.

The Walk

The curious flat top of Raasay's highest point is an immediately recognisable landmark from much of eastern Skye. Catch the ferry from Sconser as a foot passenger and then spend a day climbing to the summit and exploring the island. The walk starts from the new ferry terminal, heading along a path and roads to reach Raasay's tiny capital, Inverarish. The small terraced houses were erected in the early twentieth century as mine workers' cottages. The island's population had declined from over 900 at the beginning of the nineteenth century to only 161 in 2011. The tide has now turned, with a number of community projects and a new distillery providing some employment and attracting visitors. The walk passes the community shop, a good place to stock up on supplies and get a feel for island life.

A path through the woods passes the remains of the island's iron ore mining industry. During World War I, when iron and steel were desperately needed for the war effort, prisoners from a nearby German Prisoner of War camp were used for labour, in contravention of the Hague Convention. Such a history seems hard to comprehend as the walk winds up on to the open moorland, climbing by a burn before reaching a wild loch just below the steep flanks of Dùn Caan.

The climb up the final crags is rewarded with stunning 360-degree views of mountains, sea and islands. It's no wonder that James Boswell danced a jig when he reached the top during his 1773 tour of the Hebrides with Samuel Johnson. The descent returns over heather moorland overlooking the Cuillin. There's a carved Pictish stone before the route passes Raasay House, where Johnson and Boswell stayed during their visit. From here it's a short walk back to the pier, hopefully in time for the next ferry.

DÙN CAAN, ISLE OF RAASAY

DISTANCE: 15.5KM/9.6 MILES » **TOTAL ASCENT**: 535M/1,755FT » **START GR**: NG 545362 » **TIME**: ALLOW 6 HOURS
MAP: OS EXPLORER 409, RAASAY, RONA & SCALPAY, 1:25,000 » **REFRESHMENTS**: RAASAY HOUSE
NAVIGATION: STRAIGHTFORWARD MAP READING SKILLS REQUIRED.

LOOKING SOUTH OVER HALLAIG

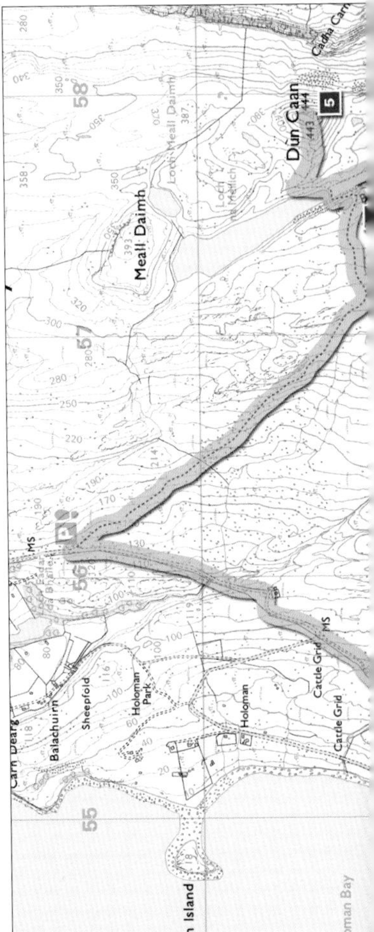

17 Dùn Caan, Isle of Raasay

Directions – Dùn Caan, Isle of Raasay

S Stepping off the ferry from Sconser, **pass to the right** of the toilet building, following the road round the back of Churchton Bay. **Turn right** on to a tarmac lane, then **keep left** at a fork, signed as a dead end. Before a gate **turn right** on to a path which soon heads left and climbs behind a bungalow. **Go through a kissing gate** and aim right across a field. Follow the path and stay on top of a bank above the coast. As the large community hall comes into view **aim right**, then **turn left on to a track** and pass in front of the hall to reach the road. **Turn right** to reach Raasay's main settlement, Inverarish.

2 **Turn left** at a junction to head uphill past the old cottages of Inverarish, originally built to house workers for the iron ore mine on the island. Pass the shop, which is well stocked and caters to visitors as well as providing a lifeline to locals. At the road junction at the top of the village **turn left then immediately right**. Shortly afterwards, **turn right** into a parking area on the site of one of the ironstone mines.

3 **Bear right** to follow a path, signed *Burma Road*. Climb up through the woodland, staying on the path ahead, and **cross a couple of footbridges**. **Turn left** on to a path signed *Dùn Cana* (the Gaelic name for Dùn Caan) which soon reaches a deer fence. **Go through the gate** and on to the open moor. **Stay on the path** as it nears another fence – ignore the stile. The path becomes faint in places and the route can be boggy; **keep left of the burn** for the next 2km. Follow the path to **pass a cairn**; the top of Dùn Caan is briefly in view.

4 Keep straight ahead to **reach Loch na Mna**, with the summit in view once more. **Keep on the lower path** that skirts the loch shore, crossing stony ground at the far end. **Keep straight on** until a clearer path joins from the right – follow this towards Loch na Meilich. **Bear right** to follow a good path diagonally uphill to the right of the loch. **Climb a series of zigzags** up the steep slopes to Dùn Caan. Take care to stay on the path to reach the rocky summit and trig point.

5 Although only 443m above sea level Dùn Caan is a classic viewpoint; the eastern coast of Skye and the Cuillin Hills provide drama on one side, while across the sea the peaks of the mainland – with the Five Sisters of Kintail prominent – look quite magnificent. **Return down the outward path** to Loch na Meilich, but this time **keep straight ahead** here to cross the shingle at the end of the loch and **climb up the escarpment beyond**.

6 At the top **follow the path** to cross the moor. After 2.1km a road is reached; **turn left along the road**. The road undulates and passes a water works. Keep **straight ahead** where another road forks right then walk for another 1km to reach a junction with an unsurfaced track.

7 **Turn right through a gate** on to the track. At the end of the track **go through a metal kissing gate** and follow a path down to the left to reach another road. **Turn left**, soon passing a carved Pictish stone on the left. Soon after this **fork right** on to a track to head towards Raasay House. At the grand mansion **turn right** on to a track leading back down to the ferry terminal road. **Keep right** at the road to return to the waiting room and – hopefully – the ferry.

TROTTERNISH COASTLINE FROM BELOW DÙN CAAN

DISTANT SGÙRR NAN GILLEAN FROM GLEN SCALADAL BAY

18 Elgol & Camasunary Circuit 17.8km/11.1 miles

This long and satisfying lower-level circuit samples some of the best of Skye's mountain and seascapes.

Camasunary car park » Am Màm pass » Camasunary Bay » Glen Scaladal » Elgol » Glasnakille » Drinan » Kilmarie » Camasunary car park

Start

Camasunary car park, B8083, Kilmarie. GR: NG 545172.

The Walk

Starting from an isolated parking area between Broadford and Elgol, the first few kilometres are up a stony track over grazing moorland, giving little hint of the fabulous landscapes to come. Once the climb to the summit of the Am Màm pass is behind you, the best of Skye is suddenly revealed ahead as the Cuillin come into view, backing Camasunary Bay and Sgùrr na Strì. The flat island of Soay, where Gavin Maxwell (author of *Ring of Bright Water*) once based an ill-fated business hunting basking sharks, can be seen with the mountains of Rùm behind.

The track descends a series of wide zigzags towards the fertile ground behind Camasunary, which means the 'bay of the white shieling'. At the coast the route turns south, passing the new bothy built in 2014, which replaced the old one on the other side of the bay. If visiting, be sure to help by carrying out any rubbish you find here.

A cliff path now leads on towards Elgol. There are two sections where it cuts across above vertiginous cliffs, and a lovely grassy bay between them. Care is needed at times, though some path improvements have been undertaken by the John Muir Trust which owns the Strathaird Estate and manages the land for both nature and community. After passing through the settlements of Elgol and Glasnakille, a mix of coastal tracks, paths and minor roads are followed to reach Kilmarie. The grand house here was once home to Jethro Tull's Ian Anderson; he was instrumental in establishing fish farming on Skye before he sold the estate to the John Muir Trust. From here it is a short walk on a minor road back to the start.

ELGOL & CAMASUNARY CIRCUIT

DISTANCE: 17.8KM/11.1 MILES » **TOTAL ASCENT**: 573M/1,880FT » **START GR**: NG 545172 » **TIME**: ALLOW 8 HOURS **MAP**: OS EXPLORER 411, SKYE: CUILLIN HILLS, 1:25,000 » **REFRESHMENTS**: ELGOL SHOP CAFE; AMY'S PLACE, TORRIN » **NAVIGATION**: STRAIGHTFORWARD; CARE NEEDED ON EXPOSED COASTAL PATH BETWEEN CAMASUNARY AND ELGOL.

ELGOL'S ROCKY BEACH

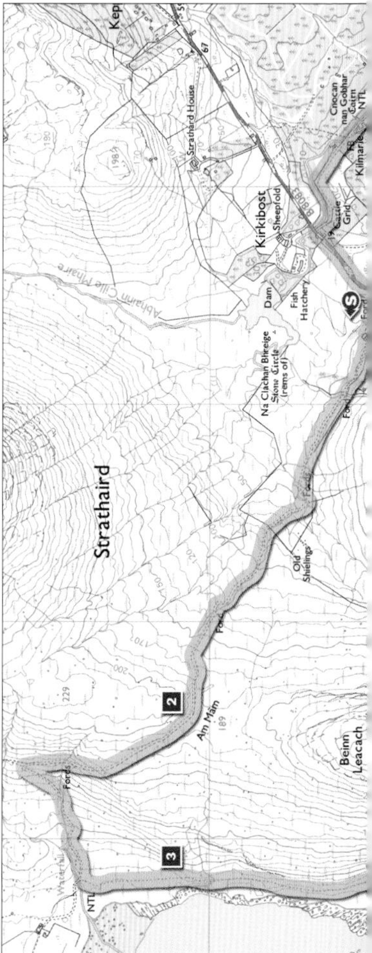

18 Elgol & Camasunary Circuit

Directions – Elgol & Camasunary Circuit

S→ From the car park **cross the road and go through the gate** on to the Camasunary track. A John Muir Trust information board gives an overview of the work of the wild land charity which manages the estate. **Follow the stony track**, crossing a couple of streams as it climbs gradually. The track dips and climbs again to eventually reach the top of the Am Màm pass. Here the Cuillin Hills are properly revealed, and there are views to the islands of Soay and Rùm out to sea.

2 **Descend the track**; the grassy sward of Camasunary Bay becomes clearer below. Stay on the narrow track as it zigzags down to the glen. Just before the bridge over the river **turn left** on to a faint path which soon leads to the new Camasunary Bothy. Built and maintained by volunteers of the Mountain Bothies Association, this two-room building has stunning views of the sea and makes a great place for a rest stop or even an overnight adventure; do carry out any rubbish.

3 From the bothy **follow the path** which heads south along the coast away from Camasunary. Climb slightly and **cross a stile** over a fence. **Head uphill on the path** and follow it as it traverses above the cliff; at times the path is very narrow and rocky with a steep drop to the sea on the right. When you can take your eyes from the path there are amazing views over Loch Scavaig to the Cuillin peaks. Around 1.5km after leaving the bothy, stay on the path as it passes over another steep drop and descend to the easier ground and the sea at Glen Scaladal.

4 Cross the small bay and **follow the path as it climbs steeply** on the far side. Stay on the path as it traverses the cliff, again with steep drops to the right in places. **Head slightly inland** on the path as the cliffs reduce in height. **Go through a gate** on to a path between fences and pass two houses. **Keep right** as the path emerges on to a lane. **Turn right** at the road and follow this steeply downhill through the scattered settlement of Elgol.

5 **Keep left** at road junction signed *Glasnakille* (it is possible to detour down to the right to visit the harbour which has celebrated views of the Cuillin Hills). Continue past the toilets and community shop which has a small cafe. **Climb gently on the road** as it heads inland and crosses moorland. The high point of the road has a mast; descend from here and cross a cattle grid to reach Glasnakille.

6 **Turn left** at a T-junction and follow the minor road past a number of croft houses. At the road end **go through a gate** and continue ahead, now on a grassy track, through woodland. **Stay on the track**; after a lonely house it becomes a surfaced road once more. Where the road bends left uphill **turn right** on to a farm track and go through two gates. Stay on the track and aim for a white cottage at Drinan. **Turn right** on to a marked path just before the cottage. Follow the path as it skirts the coast with good views to the right of the Sleat peninsula and the mountains of Knoydart beyond.

7 At a couple of houses the path emerges on to a road. **Keep straight ahead**, soon curving inland and passing Kilmarie House on the left. Stay on the road through woodland to the left of a stream to reach a junction with the B8083. **Turn left** to return along the road to the car park.

THE CUILLIN RIDGE SEEN FROM THE COAST PATH

LOOKING BACK TO BEINN NA CAILLICH FROM BEINN DEARG MHÒR

19 Broadford Red Hills 8.1km/5 miles

Rising impressively above Broadford, this cluster of three hills offers an energetic and rugged climb to the biggest cairn on Skye, rewarded with stunning views of the Cuillin, Broadford Bay and the elegant Skye Bridge.

Old Corry road end » Beinn na Caillich » col at 557 metres » Beinn Dearg Mhòr » Bealach Coire Sgreamhach » Beinn Dearg Bheag » Allt Beinn Deirge » Old Corry road end

Start

Small car park at the end of the Old Corry minor road, west of Broadford. GR: NG 619228.

The Walk

Often overlooked by walkers eager to bag the peaks of the Black Cuillin, these summits can often provide solitude as well as breathtaking 360-degree views of mountains and sea. Though lacking the scrambling of their famous neighbours, the Red Hills remain extremely steep and rugged at times; this is a far tougher walk than the distance suggests. The walk starts from a minor road end near Broadford, but there's no gentle introduction, as a faint path begins the ascent up lumpy, often boggy, ground, beyond which the going just gets ever steeper and rockier.

Eventually the gradient does ease and the giant cairn on Beinn na Caillich is reached. According to local mythology, Saucy Mary, a Norwegian princess, lies buried beneath the stones. Once resident in Castle Maol in Kyleakin, it is said that she controlled the narrows between Skye and the mainland and thanked passing sailors that paid her toll by flashing her breasts, hence her name. In 1772 the noted traveller Thomas Pennant made the ascent, the first recorded of a Skye mountain. He was more impressed by the view in the opposite direction, writing 'The prospect to the west was of desolation itself; a savage series of rude mountains, discoloured, black and red, as if by the rage of fire.'

The walk continues along a ridge with Pennant's view of the Cuillin ahead, and the Small Isles well seen to the left. A brief descent to a bealach is followed by the straightforward climb to the second peak of the day, Beinn Dearg Mhòr. From here the next descent is much trickier, with steep screes to negotiate, before an easier climb to the final summit, Beinn Dearg Bheag. A broad ridge for the descent completes the horseshoe followed by a final slog over boggy moorland to return to the start.

BROADFORD RED HILLS

DISTANCE: 8.1KM/5 MILES » **TOTAL ASCENT**: 984M/3,228FT » **START GR**: NG 619228 » **TIME**: ALLOW 6 HOURS
MAP: OS EXPLORER 411, SKYE: CUILLIN HILLS, 1:25,000 » **REFRESHMENTS**: CAFE SIA OR DELI GASTA, BROADFORD
NAVIGATION: GOOD MAP READING SKILLS ESSENTIAL.

Directions – Broadford Red Hills

Just west of Broadford a minor road leaves the A87, signed *Old Corry*. There is limited parking near the end of the road, but do not block the turning circle; there is some more space back towards the houses at Old Corry. **Take the very faint footpath** opposite the house at the road end to head north-west directly towards Beinn na Caillich. The going is boggy and rough underfoot. **Follow the burn** as the route starts climbing uphill. The climb is unrelenting and becomes increasingly rocky as the ground steepens. **Keep heading uphill**; aiming to pass to the left of a prominent rocky outcrop. Regular stops allow the view behind to be appreciated as the islands of the Inner Sound and Applecross hills open up to the east.

2 Once past the stones, **climb the final grassy slope** to reach the summit of Beinn na Caillich, the highest of the day at 732m. Looking west, the mountain of Blàbheinn is prominent with the serrated main Cuillin peaks beyond. From the cairn, **walk past the trig point and descend the ridge**, aiming south-west towards the col between Beinn na Caillich and Beinn Dearg Mhòr. **Continue beyond the lowest point** at 557m to **start the climb** up to the second peak. There are excellent views, and it is much easier going than the initial climb.

3 The easier going is short lived: from the summit cairn (709m) **walk south-east** to descend steep screes to Bealach Coire Sgreamhach, which translates as the 'pass of the scree'. **Follow one of the many loose paths down** through the steep scree, **keeping just right of the actual ridge** to find the easiest line.

VIEW TO RÙM

4 **Continue straight on** from the bealach, now on easier ground, to climb up the ridge. **Follow the path up** the rocky slope to soon reach the summit cairn of Beinn Dearg Bheag at 582m.

5 From this final peak of the day **descend the broad ridge**, aiming south-east and then east, to follow the final part of the horseshoe. **Keep heading downhill**; once almost at the end of the ridge **bear left** to descend boggy ground. Continue on to **cross the Allt Beinn Deirge** – straightforward unless in spate. The house at the road end can now be seen to the north-east; **aim directly towards the house**. **Cross a small stream** and soon emerge at the road end and the start of the walk.

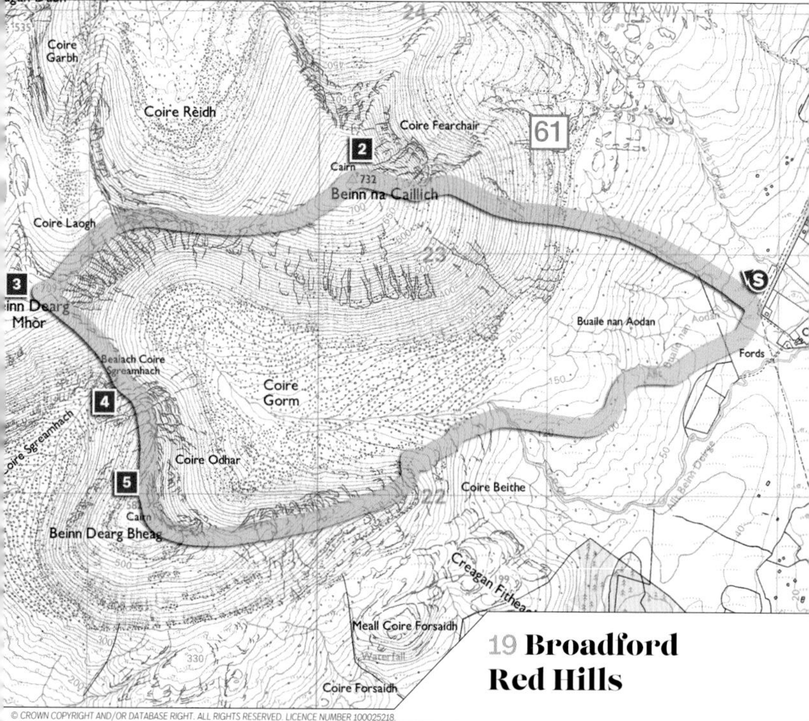

THE CUILLIN RIDGE FROM BLÀBHEINN SUMMIT

20 Blàbheinn

7.8km/4.8 miles

Standing apart from the main Cuillin Ridge, Blàbheinn is a challenging ascent for experienced hillwalkers, offering a truly stunning view of the other Black Cuillin peaks.

Blàbheinn car park » Allt na Dunaiche » Coire Uaigneich » Blàbheinn east ridge » Blàbheinn summit » Blàbheinn east ridge » Coire Uaigneich » Allt na Dunaiche » Blàbheinn car park

Start

Blàbheinn car park, B8083, western side of Loch Slapin. GR: NG 560216.

The Walk

The only one of the Black Cuillin to stand apart from the main ridge, Blàbheinn rises majestically above the waters of Loch Slapin, and ranks among the finest mountains in Britain. While the ascent is short in distance and is sometimes described as an 'easy' Skye Munro, the upper half is very rocky and rugged, and the easiest way is less than obvious – good navigation and route-finding skills are needed.

From the car park on the western shore of Loch Slapin, a path follows a tumbling burn up into Coire Uaigneich between Blàbheinn and An Stac. Up to this point the climb is steady but straightforward, but as the path nears the grassy bowl of the upper coire things become trickier as clear paths are left behind for the steep ascent of the mountain's eastern flank. This is steep and loose with scree in places and needs care as well as lung power. Eventually the gradient eases off and the route skirts around above dramatic cliffs, with views over to Clach Glas – a neighbouring peak often known as the Matterhorn of Skye.

The unforgettable summit views are revealed at the last moment, as the main Cuillin Ridge is seen in its entirety across the great gulf of Glen Sligachan – a view given great depth by the crags falling away at your feet. The combination of Blàbheinn with Clach Glas is a classic mountaineering route requiring rock-climbing skills, while even the short traverse to the south summit requires some trickier scrambling, so the only straightforward descent is to retrace your steps.

BLÀBHEINN

DISTANCE: 7.8KM/4.8 MILES » **TOTAL ASCENT**: 900M/2,953FT » **START GR**: NG 560216 » **TIME**: ALLOW 6 HOURS
MAP: OS EXPLORER 411, SKYE: CUILLIN HILLS, 1:25,000 » **REFRESHMENTS**: AMY'S PLACE, TORRIN
NAVIGATION: CAREFUL ROUTE FINDING NEEDED ON HIGHER PATHLESS SECTIONS; TRICKY IN POOR WEATHER.

Directions – Blàbheinn

S Take the B8083 from Broadford and, after rounding the northern end of Loch Slapin, look out for the signed car park on the right. Maintained by the John Muir Trust, the wild land charity which owns and manages the mountain and its surroundings, there is an information board and toilets. **Take the path from the far end of the car park**; **bear right** through rowan trees and down alongside the burn to reach the road. **Turn left** to cross the water and immediately on the far side **turn left** again on to a path. Follow the clear path as it climbs up next to a steep, wooded gorge. **Go through two gates** and keep following the path on to open moorland. **Stay on the path**, climbing uphill and passing a couple of waterfalls with Blàbheinn visible beyond. Soon you can look into a second gorge carved by the Allt na Dunaiche.

2 Eventually the path crosses this stream and then another; **continue heading uphill**. The ground becomes increasingly rocky. Keep climbing, soon reaching Coire Uaigneich with the steep walls of An Stac on the left and Blàbheinn ahead and to the right. As the ground begins to widen out into the grassy bowl of Fionna-choire, **turn sharp right. There is no obvious path** – if you reach a massive boulder, you've gone too far.

3 There is no one clear path at first; past the edge of the cliffs **bear right and zigzag up the steep slope**. Eventually the ground becomes more scree-covered and there is a faint zigzag path which makes the going easier. Keep a close eye on the map, especially in poor weather, and **keep working your way up the open, rocky slope**. Higher up, **climb a narrow scree gully** to gain access to the final part of the climb. Once past the steepest ground **bear left**, with the route becoming clearer and heading towards the rim of Blàbheinn's eastern cliffs. **Head up the slope to the left** as jaw-dropping views of the Great Prow are revealed in the gaps between the buttresses. **Pass a cairn** with a good view of the pointed peak of Clach Glas. **Keep heading uphill**; the route becomes increasingly rocky and eventually heads up a rocky gully. **Scramble out of the top of the gully** or climb the rocks on the left. **Continue ahead** to reach the summit of Blàbheinn.

4 At 928m this is the only Skye Munro that is not on the main Cuillin Ridge. This makes it a unique viewpoint, and it's worth spending a while picking out the mountains seen across Glen Sligachan. On a clear day much of Skye can be made out as well as the Isle of Raasay, the west coast of the mainland and the Small Isles. While it is possible to head south-west for the scramble up to the slightly lower south top and descend this ridge, the scramble to this top is trickier than anything on the route described here, and the ridge leads far from the start. The best descent route therefore is to **retrace your outward route**.

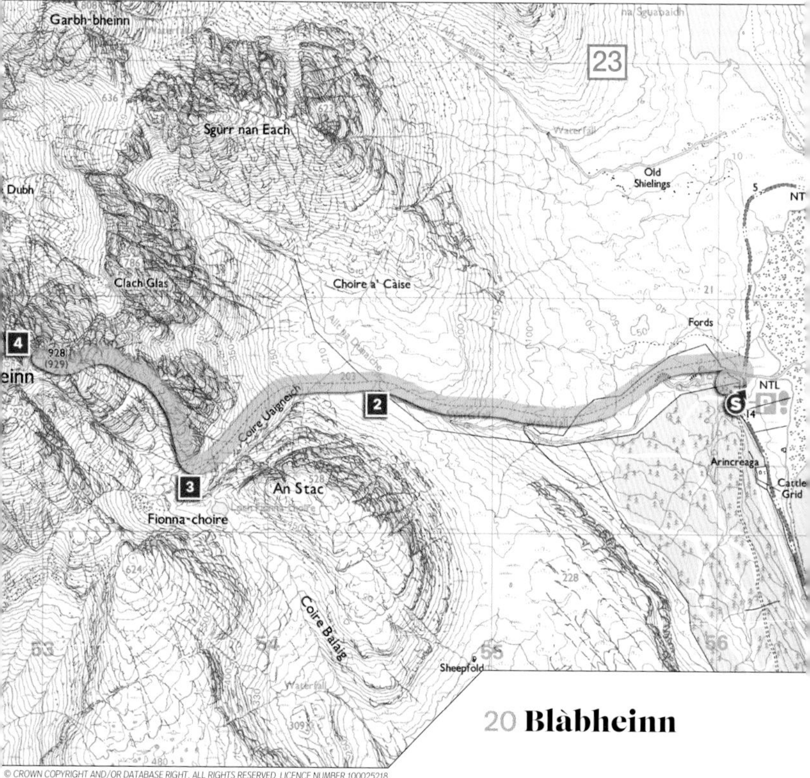

20 Blàbheinn

Appendix

The following is a list of shops, cafes, pubs, websites and other contacts that might come in handy.

VISITOR INFORMATION CENTRES

Portree . . . . T: **01478 612 992**

FOOD AND DRINK

Cafes

Amy's Place, Torrin . . . . T: **01471 822 847**
Aros Centre, near Portree . T: **01478 613 750**
Blas Cafe, Dunvegan . . . . . . T: **01470 521 841**
Cafe 1925, Ardvasar . . . . . . T: **01471 844 255**
Cafe Arriba, Portree . . . . T: **01478 611 830**
Cafe Sia, Broadford . . . . T: **01471 822 616**
Columba 1400, Staffin . . . . T: **01478 611 410**
Deli Gasta, Broadford . . . . T: **01471 822 646**
Elgol Shop Cafe . . . . T: **01471 866 329**
Glenbrittle Campsite Cafe . . T: **01478 640 404**
Raasay House, ... T: **01478 660 300**
Isle of Raasay
Storr View Coffee,
Near Old Man of Storr Car Park
The Dunvegan Deli-Cafe, . . T: **01470 521 497**
Dunvegan

Pubs

Sligachan Hotel . . . . T: **01478 650 358**
Taigh Ailean Hotel, ... T: **01478 640 271**
Portnalong
Uig Hotel, Uig . . . . T: **01470 542 205**

ACCOMMODATION

B&Bs, hotels & campsites

www.visitscotland.com
www.walkhighlands.co.uk/skye

Hostels & bunkhouses

www.hostellingscotland.org.uk
www.hostel-scotland.co.uk

Bothies

www.mountainbothies.org.uk

PUBLIC TRANSPORT

www.calmac.co.uk
www.stagecoachbus.com

WEATHER

www.mwis.org.uk
www.metoffice.gov.uk
www.smidgeup.com/midge-forecast

OTHER CONTACTS

www.outdooraccess-scotland.scot
www.nature.scot/enjoying-outdoors

OUTDOOR SHOPS

Inside Out . . . . T: **01478 611 663**
Portree, **www.inside-out-skye.com**

Cioch Outdoor . . . . T: **01470 572 707**
Clothing Company
Struan, **www.cioch-direct.co.uk**

OTHER PUBLICATIONS

Scottish Island Bagging
Helen & Paul Webster, Vertebrate Publishing
www.v-publishing.co.uk

Day Walks in Fort William & Glen Coe
Helen & Paul Webster, Vertebrate Publishing
www.v-publishing.co.uk

Day Walks in the Cairngorms
Helen & Paul Webster, Vertebrate Publishing
www.v-publishing.co.uk

Day Walks in Northumberland
David Wilson, Vertebrate Publishing
www.v-publishing.co.uk

Big Trails: Great Britain & Ireland
Edited by Kathy Rogers & Stephen Ross, Vertebrate Publishing
www.v-publishing.co.uk

RAASAY FERRY

THE CUILLIN SEEN FROM GESTO

ABOUT THE AUTHORS

Helen and Paul Webster share a passion for walking and wild places. In 2003–2004 they undertook a life-changing 4,000-mile continuous backpacking trip across Europe. Following their return, they quit their careers to begin a new life evangelising for Scotland's spectacular outdoors – especially the Highlands and Islands. Together they set up Walkhighlands, a free online guide and forum which has become the busiest walkers' website in the UK. They have also written nineteen guide-books to various areas of Scotland, including *Scottish Island Bagging*, and in 2018 Paul won the Scottish Landscape Photographer of the Year competition. They live in the Cairngorms National Park.
www.walkhighlands.co.uk

VERTEBRATE PUBLISHING

At Vertebrate Publishing we publish books to inspire adventure.

It's our rule that the only books we publish are those that we'd want to read or use ourselves. We endeavour to bring you beautiful books that stand the test of time and that you'll be proud to have on your bookshelf for years to come.

The Peak District was the inspiration behind our first books. Our offices are situated on its doorstep, minutes away from world-class climbing, biking and hillwalking. We're driven by our own passion for the outdoors, for exploration, and for the natural world; it's this passion that we want to share with our readers.

We aim to inspire everyone to get out there. We want to connect readers – young and old – with the outdoors and the positive impact it can have on well-being. We think it's particularly important that young people get outside and explore the natural world, something we support through our publishing programme.

As well as publishing award-winning new books, we're working to make available many out-of-print classics in both print and digital formats. These are stories that we believe are unique and significant; we want to make sure that they continue to be shared and enjoyed.
www.v-publishing.co.uk